T0079689

MELON

Edible

Series Editor: Andrew F. Smith

EDIBLE is a revolutionary series of books dedicated to food and drink that explores the rich history of cuisine. Each book reveals the global history and culture of one type of food or beverage.

Already published

Apple Erika Janik *Banana* Lorna Piatti-Farnell
Barbecue Jonathan Deutsch and Megan J. Elias
Beef Lorna Piatti-Farnell *Beer* Gavin D. Smith
Brandy Becky Sue Epstein *Bread* William Rubel
Cake Nicola Humble *Caviar* Nichola Fletcher
Champagne Becky Sue Epstein *Cheese* Andrew Dalby
Chocolate Sarah Moss and Alexander Badenoch
Cocktails Joseph M. Carlin *Curry* Colleen Taylor Sen
Dates Nawal Nasrallah *Doughnut* Heather Delancey Hunwick
Dumplings Barbara Gallani *Eggs* Diane Toops
Fats Michelle Phillipov *Figs* David C. Sutton
Game Paula Young Lee *Gin* Lesley Jacobs Solmonson
Hamburger Andrew F. Smith *Herbs* Gary Allen
Hot Dog Bruce Kraig *Ice Cream* Laura B. Weiss
Lamb Brian Yarvin *Lemon* Toby Sonneman
Lobster Elisabeth Townsend *Melon* Sylvia Lovegren
Milk Hannah Velten *Mushroom* Cynthia D. Bertelsen
Nuts Ken Albala *Offal* Nina Edwards *Olive* Fabrizia Lanza
Onions and Garlic Martha Jay *Oranges* Clarissa Hyman
Pancake Ken Albala *Pie* Janet Clarkson
Pineapple Kaori O' Connor *Pizza* Carol Helstosky
Pork Katharine M. Rogers *Potato* Andrew F. Smith
Pudding Jeri Quinzio *Rice* Renee Marton *Rum* Richard Foss
Salmon Nicolaas Mink *Sandwich* Bee Wilson
Sauces Maryann Tebben *Sausage* Gary Allen *Soup* Janet Clarkson
Spices Fred Czarra *Sugar* Andrew F. Smith *Tea* Helen Saberi
Tequila Ian Williams *Truffle* Zachary Nowak
Vodka Patricia Herlihy *Water* Ian Miller
Whiskey Kevin R. Kosar *Wine* Marc Millon

Melon

A Global History

Sylvia Lovegren

REAKTION BOOKS

Published by Reaktion Books Ltd
Unit 32, Waterside
44–48 Wharf Road
London N1 7UK
www.reaktionbooks.co.uk

First published 2016

Printed and bound in China by 1010 Printing International Ltd

A catalogue record for this book is available
from the British Library

ISBN 978 1 78023 584 4

Contents

Introduction

Whenever you eat fruit, eat melon, because it is the fruit of
Paradise and contains a thousand blessings and a thousand mercies.
Attributed to the Prophet Mohammed

Last summer my husband came home from the market with
an unusual melon, the Hami, named for the oasis on the exotic Silk Road in Central Asia, where it was developed. It was a
golden-green oval with slightly wrinkly skin, about the size
of a standard muskmelon. Curious about the taste of this
new-to-us melon, we cut it open right away. We were completely unprepared for the experience awaiting us. It's hard
to say whether or not this was the most delicious thing we
had ever eaten, but it was without a doubt the most exquisite.
The taste is hard to describe, but if you can imagine a combination of honey, attar of roses and jasmine with an intense
yet clean and not musky melon flavour, you'd come close to
the taste of that melon, all wrapped up in tender, melting,
silky flesh. It was unbelievably good, the apotheosis of melon.
We hoarded that Hami melon, doling out little bits to each
other and our closest friends and family members. The experi -
ence of eating it was so rich that a small taste was all that was
needed. When it was at last gone, we saved up our pennies –

it was an expensive melon – and bought another. The second Hami melon was a crushing disappointment: it tasted like any other generic supermarket melon. Hami melon number three had a hint of the exquisite perfume and flavour of Hami melon number one, just enough to frustrate us, but not enough to satisfy. We had had our taste of Paradise and it was, apparently, not to be repeated.

Then, a few weeks later, I spotted a strange-looking melon in the market. It resembled a shaggy cucumber, its oddly wrinkled skin an intense, almost glowing dark lime green. It appeared to be something out of a scene from *Star Trek*. This strange fruit was a karella, or bitter melon, very popular with the Indian and Caribbean immigrants in the neighbourhood. I vaguely remembered tasting bitter melon in a soup – Chinese, perhaps? – many years ago, and thought it would be fun to try something new. A quick search provided a number of recipes, most of them involving Indian or East Asian techniques, but one recipe appealed, a simple stir-fry with garlic and onion, preceded by a soak in salted water to 'draw out the bitterness'. Slicing the melon into the brine – the scalloped pieces so appealing and unusual – I nibbled one pretty slice. It was bitter, yes, but with a bright snap and fresh vegetal taste: not bad at all, I thought. Different, but quite edible. When the time came, I sautéed the bitter melon with the aromatics and turned it out into a serving dish. The pretty scalloped pieces of melon were attractively tangled with the soft onion and golden bits of rich garlic and the whole thing looked quite appetizing, if unusual. One bite, however, was all it took: I have never literally spat food out of my mouth before, but that first bite of bitter melon went in and came out, no swallowing involved. The taste was like – well, imagine biting into a piece of garlic-flavoured poison, with a heavy metallic edge. Ghastly. My husband, on the other hand, honestly *liked* the bitter melon and polished off the entire bowlful with great pleasure, then asked rather wistfully if I might consider making it again sometime, just for him.

Here were two very different foods – one sweet and fruity, the other bitter and vegetal – but both known as melons not only in popular usage but botanically. I can't think of any other common fruit or vegetable that has a comparable diversity of taste and usage. Apples? Asparagus? Potatoes? Onions? Figs? Broccoli?

The melon tribe is simply an enormous one, diverse in taste, geographic range and appearance, ranging from the common sweet melons popular the world over – watermelons, canta - loupes and honeydew melons – to vegetable melons, such as my bitter melon, pickling melons, cucumber-like 'snake' melons and the courgette-like green melons popular in Asia but now gaining commerce in the West. There are also many melons that are not generally well known, such as the wild tsamma melons so important to the /Gwi San people in the Kalahari desert, the egusi seed melons common in Nigeria, the bitter medicinal colocynth watermelons that were used extensively in antiquity but have largely fallen by the way-side in modern times, and the mostly inedible but highly scented Queen Anne's pocket melons, among many others. Genetic diversity in melons is common and scientists estimate the number of melon cultivars to be in the hundreds – and possibly thousands.

One reason for the great diversity in the melon family is its age and broad range. Molecular-clock dating suggests that the Asian ancestor of one type of melon diverged from its African relatives during the Miocene period some 12 million years ago. In more comprehensible human terms, the oldest melon family remains were excavated in Thailand, and dated to approximately 10,000 BC. Scientists believe that melons

Melons and watermelons at a market in Ukraine.

were already being domesticated by at least 7000–3000 BC in Asia and Africa. And it is in those two areas – the first areas populated by *Homo sapiens* – that scientists think that most melons got their start as a popular food.

How and why and when these various melons – particularly watermelons and sweet melons – spread from their ancestral homes will be the focus of this book. Along the way, we'll examine some of the difficulties in tracing the roads these melons took and how scientists and historians have dealt with these difficulties. This really is a mystery story with clues scattered throughout the globe and across thousands of years. Some of the mysteries have been solved; many others are still waiting for the final clues to be discovered and answers revealed.

One problem with identifying melons in history is that so many of them look not only like other melons, but like other members of the larger squash family to which melons belong. If we're lucky enough to find an ancient painting or sculpture of a 'melon' it is very difficult to work out exactly what the artist was actually depicting. Sometimes the ancient painting or sculpture may be 'proof' that a particular kind of melon existed in that time and that place, but not always. For example, there is an ancient Egyptian tomb painting that seems to show a watermelon. But does it? Or is it more likely the related and very similar looking colocynth melon? Most scholars at this point think it is indeed a watermelon, but there is a vocal minority who say it couldn't possibly be. No one has yet been able to demonstrate how watermelons got from western Africa to Egypt, so perhaps that vocal minority has a point – or not. In addition there are artefacts from Egypt as well as ancient Greece and Rome that show what have for years been identified as cucumbers, but new scholarly research indicates that all those images of and references to so-called

A variety of different watermelons.

A melon from George Brookshaw's *Pomona Britannica* (1817).

cucumbers in ancient documents very likely show a type of vegetable melon popular in the area in ancient times that has mostly disappeared from modern agriculture.

Speaking of vegetable melons and cucumbers leads us to another difficulty in tracing the secret history of melons: like most produce, melons are very biodegradable. Except for a piece of what appears to be a section of watermelon rind unearthed in South Africa dating back some 5,000 years, most of the few melon remains that have been excavated from ancient sites are seeds. The problem with 'melon' seeds is that they can be from sweet melons, vegetable melons or even cucumbers – and the difference between the seeds can only be spotted by using high-tech laboratory equipment. If those early archaeological seed finds are still available to modern scientists, perhaps one day they will be examined. In the meantime we don't know what kind of seeds they are. Watermelon seeds are more distinctive, yet it is very hard to distinguish between the seeds of the common sweet watermelon and those of the bitter colocynth or the wild tsamma melon. So archaeology can give us some clues in solving our historic mystery puzzle, but often cannot solve the puzzle by itself.

Another great difficulty in understanding early mentions of melons – both in ancient and medieval times – is that the names used for melons and their family members overlap, contradict each other and change over time. Just as ancient 'cucumbers' may actually be a kind of melon, so may the names given to members of the melon in different periods obfuscate rather than illuminate. Trying to trace these various names is extremely challenging, but it is one of the primary tools scholars have to understand early melon history.

While unravelling melons' tangled history may be difficult at times, eating and appreciating these delicious fruits is not. King Tutankhamun in ancient Egypt apparently ate them, the first Moghul emperor of India is supposed to have wept copiously over a dish of melons simply because of the taste, and a famous pope is said to have died from a surfeit of melon. Today millions of people across the globe enjoy melons, one of the most widely grown and well-known warm-weather fruits. Melons span time and geography, but they cross class and cultural boundaries as well: delicious wild melons grow

Grilled watermelon 'steak', a trendy modern dish.

free for the picking in the sandy wastes of the Kalahari Desert, while cosseted melons are grown in specially enriched soil in square glass containers in Japan before they are picked, decorated and sold in custom-made boxes for the equivalent of U.S.$100.

I

Getting to Know Melons

Men and melons are hard to know.

Benjamin Franklin

Most fruits – such as, say, apples – don't really need much in-depth identification because the different varieties resemble each other so closely, but the melon tribe is large and diverse. So let's begin with the actual botanical dictionary definition of the melon.

Like their relatives the courgette (zucchini), pumpkin, gourd, cucumber, squash and loofah, melons are members of the huge Cucurbitaceae family, all of which may be referred to as 'cucurbits'. Watermelons and melons, along with cucumbers and some gourds, are native to the Old World. Their relatives – zucchini/courgette, summer squash, pumpkins, marrows and winter squash, along with other types of gourd – are native to the New World. This is very important to remember because, as we go through the historical record, we'll find all kinds of references to 'pumpkins' and 'squash' in Europe before Columbus, which – since pumpkins and squash are native to the New World – we know is not possible.

Melon plants are (mostly) frost-sensitive annual vines. The fleshy fruits – the melons and watermelons that we eat – are a type of modified berry. The fruit of sweet melons is bland when the melon is immature, only developing sugars and a sweet flavour at the end of the ripening period and only under the right circumstances of enough sun and not too much moisture. In the Cucurbitaceae family, there are two branches or genera that we usually associate with melons: *Citrullus* (watermelon) and *Cucumis* (sweet melon and some vegetable melons as well). Both of these major types will be the focus of this book – the two basic types we in the West think of when we say 'melon'.

Watermelons: *Citrullus lanatus*

The 'green whale of summer', as poet Pablo Neruda wonderfully described it, is *Citrullus lanatus*, the common watermelon. Its smooth green skin and deliciously sweet red, yellow or sometimes cream flesh with its beguilingly icy texture has made it one of the most recognized and popular fruits around the world. *C. lanatus* includes the egusi melon, grown primarily for its nutritious seeds. The *Citrullus* genus also contains *C. colocynthis*, or the colocynth, a bitter, not very edible melon much used as a medicine in ancient times and a perennial vine; and *C. ecirrhosus* or the tsamma melon, another perennial that grows wild in Namibia and South Africa and which is valued not only for its seeds but for the water stored in its flesh. All species in the *Citrullus* genus will interbreed, and all look very much like the common watermelon. Recent research shows that the citron melon, whose thick skin is used in candying, is not, after all, a *C. lanatus* but is more distantly related to it than was once thought.

Sweet Melons: *Cucumis melo*

The *Cucumis* genus also includes cucumbers and gherkins, but we'll only be looking at the melons in this group, all of which are classified as *Cucumis melo*. There are many different kinds of *C. melo*, including cantaloupes, honeydew melons and muskmelons, and scientists have grappled with different taxonomic groupings over the years. Because of the tangled history of melons and because any *C. melo* type will interbreed with any other *C. melo* type, trying to keep the groupings straight has been difficult. There are long-standing arguments in the scientific community about the number of divisions that should be listed under *C. melo*, but here we will look at seven groups (plus some stragglers).

C. melo var. *cantaloupensis* includes European cantaloupes such as the Charentais melon, the galia melon and the Algerian melon. Just to confuse us, it does *not* include the North American 'cantaloupe', which is technically a member of *reticulatus*

European cantaloupes showing typical pronounced ribbing.

(see below). The melons are generally round in shape and often quite ribbed, with either smooth or knobbly skin. They have a pronounced perfume, usually have orange flesh, and the fruit does not slip from the vine when mature.

C. melo var. *reticulatus* includes muskmelons, nutmeg melons and Persian melons. The three most prominent characteristics of this group are the musky odour of the sweet flesh and the netted skin of the melon – in fact, the French describe these melons as 'embroidered' because of the designs on the skin. The last important difference is the fact that the melon 'slips' from the vine when it is ripe, something most other melons – or cucurbits – do not do. The fruits are round or oval and can have orange, cream, or green flesh. The netted fruit that Americans and Canadians call 'cantaloupe' is actually a muskmelon.

C. melo var. *inodorus* includes honeydew (also called white Antibes), Crenshaw, Santa Claus, canary, casaba, piel de sapo, Hami and Christmas melons, among others. These delicious

Muskmelons or rock melons, known as cantaloupes in North America.

Inodorus melons for sale in Germany.

melons have either smooth or warty but not netted skin, are either round or oblong in shape, have exceptionally sweet flesh – when well-grown and ripe – that is often green or white but can occasionally be orange, and have very light to no odour, which is why they are labelled *in-ODOR-us*. Most do not slip off the vine at maturity but a few of the newer cultivars do. *Inodorus* melons tend to be somewhat larger than other *C. melo* varieties and take longer to grow. Because of their late maturity and because they can be stored for a few weeks to a few months after picking, they are often confusingly known as 'winter melons', a name also given to a vegetable melon (*Benincasa hispida*) common in Asia.

Snake or serpent melons and the 'Armenian cucumber' make up *C. melo* var. *flexuosus*. As you may guess from the name, the fruits of this melon are long and thin, either straight

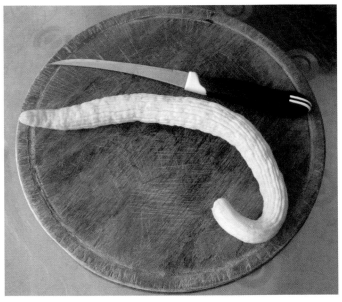

A snake melon ready to be sliced for a salad.

Korean striped conomon melons.

or curled in a most snake-like manner, with light- or dark-green ribbed or striped skin. The flesh is not sweet, but is very crisp, refreshing and cucumberish. These melons are generally treated as vegetables. Their similarity in looks and taste to cucumbers, along with their popularity in the ancient Near East, has caused much confusion among historians, botanists and linguists over the years, as we will see later.

The conomon group of melons (pickling melons) is just now becoming known in the West but *C. melo* var. *conomon* has been grown and appreciated in Asia for thousands of years. Conomons are not usually sweet and with their crisp flesh and smooth skins they are primarily used as pickling melons. The fruit can be globular or cylindrical, and may be green, yellow, white or striped.

Perfume melons make up a very small group – *C. melo* var. *dudaim* – also sometimes called *Cucumis aromaticus*. The round or oval fruits have crisp, bland or bitter flesh that only the very hungry would eat, but these small striped fruits offer a delicious perfume. They were supposedly carried by Queen Anne of England, Scotland and Ireland (*r.* 1702–14) to sweeten the air around her, hence the common name 'Queen Anne's pocket melon'. It is also known as Dudaim melon, apple melon, vine pomegranate, plum granny and wild muskmelon (the last name indicates its weedy and competitive habit, which can make them *melona non grata* to commercial melon growers).

Another melon that has been grown in India and Asia for thousands of years but is only now becoming known in the West, *C. melo* var. *momordica*, consists of the snap or phut melon. The fruits are oval or cylindrical with smooth skin. The flesh is dry and mealy and usually eaten, either cooked or raw, when the melon is still young and tender. The name 'phut' comes from the Hindi word *phutna*, to split, which is exactly what this melon does when it ripens.

Plum granny melons beguile with their looks as well as their sweet odour.

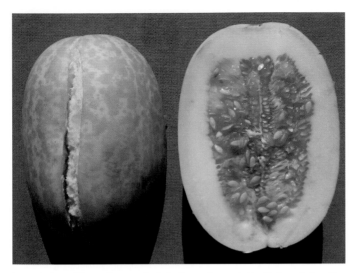
Snap melons. The melon on the left shows the typical splitting of the skin that indicates maturity.

Also belonging to *Cucumis melo* but not included in the seven groups above are chito melons, which are frequently known as garden lemons, melon apples, vine peaches, mango melons or orange melons. These descriptive names might make you think that chito melons are sweet and aromatic, but the names reflect only the melon's physical appearance. This melon has been used for pickling, and pickled melons in North America were called, confusingly enough, 'mangoes', hence the name 'mango melon'. Chito melons are small and round and look very much like mini cantaloupes, but the taste is more cucumber than cantaloupe (although some chitos are sweeter than others).

And finally there is the chate melon, a cucumber-ish sort of fruit that is usually harvested and eaten while immature. It is infrequently grown now but was common around the Mediterranean and in the Middle East during the time of the

Chate melons in an Italian market.

Pharaohs and the ancient Sumerians, and its use has caused headaches for historians, botanists and linguists ever since. We will hear more about *C. melo* var. *chate* when we examine the history of melons in the ancient world.

Bitter Melon and Winter Melon

In addition to *Citrullus lanatus* and *Cucumis melo*, the culinary world of melons and the Cucurbitaceae family also includes the bitter melon (*Momordica charantia*) and the winter melon (*Benincasa hispida*) – not to be confused with the *C. melo* 'winter melon'.

The bitter melon, *Momordica charantia* – sometimes also known as the bitter gourd or the bitter cucumber, leprosy gourd, balsam pear or karella – is, not surprisingly, very bitter to the taste. This is because it contains a high level of cucurbitacin, one of the bitterest chemicals known to man. Bitter melon grows throughout Asia, Africa and the Caribbean, and looks something like a very warty – or even shaggy – cucumber. Scientists believe that this melon originated in southeastern Asia and that it has been grown for thousands of years: the prehistoric inhabitants of India had a name for it which would become the modern 'karella'. It is generally eaten while still young since the bitterness increases as the fruit matures, and it is primarily cooked as a vegetable, although it is occasionally eaten raw in salads.

Benincasa hispida, or the winter melon, is also known as the wax gourd, the Chinese winter melon, the Chinese preserving melon, the fuzzy or hairy gourd and the ash pumpkin. The fruit is large and oblong, with green skin that develops a waxy bloom as it matures. Winter melon is somewhat sweet and bland. It is popular throughout tropical Asia as a cooked vegetable and is also candied and used in drinks. It has been grown in Southeast Asia, where it originated, for over 2,000 years. The thick, waxy skin of the mature winter melon makes it ideal for keeping and it can be stored for up to a year after it is picked.

In this book we will focus primarily on the Prophet's two basic 'fruits of Paradise': watermelon and the familiar sweet melon, such as honeydew, cantaloupe and muskmelon. The story of how these melons spread from their homelands in Africa and Asia to the farthest corners of the world is the story of the explorers, travellers, brigands, slaves, slavers, farmers, conquerors and missionaries who carried melon seeds – and the memory of the luscious melons they had eaten – with them around the world and, in so doing, changed history. Along the way, we will also encounter some of the vegetable melons mentioned above, some of whose histories are inextricably intertwined with the sweet melons, and others of which

Bitter melon, *Momordica charantia*.

Winter melons growing in the Philippines.

are just beginning to make an impact upon the world stage. And we will observe scientists, archaeologists, historians, linguists and other scholars as they try to solve the mystery of the origins and travels of the melon.

2

Melons in Prehistory and the Ancient World

[The melon is] a fruit whose history, varieties, and
nomenclature perplex even experts.
'Melon', in *Oxford Companion to Food*

Perfumed, sweet, succulent, cooling, a ripe melon can be one
of the most swooningly delicious of fruits, with a long and
deliciously exotic history to match. And humans have been
eating and enjoying melons for thousands of years. But which
humans? Where? And which melons? Trying to untangle that
exotic history has been difficult to do – until recently. For
years the scientific and historical consensus seemed to be that
watermelons and sweet melons got their start in either Africa
or India, but no one was really sure which.

Botanists had long been puzzled by watermelon's origins.
Many were convinced that the fruit had dispersed from its
unknown homeland in the far distant past partly because of
the enormous diversity of watermelon names: the ancient
Egyptian word for watermelon is *bddw-k*, which became the
Coptic *betuke*, the Hebrew *avattihim* and the Arabic *battikh-al-
sindi* (or *al-hindi*). The Persians call watermelons *hinduwani*, the
Italians *cocomero* or *anguria*, the Spanish *sandia*, the French
pastèque, the Portuguese *melancia* and the Turkish *karpuz*. All

of these names seem distinct and unrelated linguistically, supporting the idea that watermelon spread over Europe and the Near East very early. But a bit of investigation reveals that the diversity of names for watermelon is easily explainable: the Italian *cocomero* is a variation on the Latin word for cucumber, and *anguria* probably comes from a Byzantine Greek word for cucumber as well. The Spanish *sandia* comes from the last part of Arabic *battikh-al-sindi*, while the French *pastèque* is descended more obviously from *battikh*. The Portuguese *melancia* appears to come from 'melon' and the Turks took *karpuz* from the Persian word for sweet melon. What at first appears to be a veritable Tower of Babel of names for the homely watermelon is, upon closer examination, not so remarkable after all.

Many scientists thought watermelon came from India, where it naturalized freely in the deserts, though they were surprised to find no wild species there. Still, some names for watermelon hinted at an Indian origin, like the medieval Arabic *battikh-al-sindi* (or *al-hindi*), and the Persian *hinduwani*. Linnaeus

Watermelons in a market in Tallinn, Estonia.

thought watermelon was from southern Italy and the great eighteenth-century Swiss botanist Alphonse Pyramus de Candolle thought southern Asia. And then in 1858 the British explorer David Livingstone looked out over the African Kalahari Desert and unwittingly made scientific history. He wrote in his diary:

> But the most surprising plant of the Desert is the Kengwe or Keme' (*Cucumis caffer*), the watermelon. In years when more than the usual quantity of rain falls, vast tracts of the country are literally covered with these melons . . . Then animals of every sort and name, including man, rejoice in the rich supply . . . These melons are not, however, all of them eatable; some are sweet, and others so bitter that the whole are named by the Boers the bitter watermelon. The natives select them by striking one melon after another with a hatchet, and applying the tongue to the gashes. They thus readily distinguish between the bitter and sweet. The bitter are deleterious, but the sweet are quite wholesome.

Livingstone's observation directed scientists' attention to Africa as the cradle of the watermelon, with most agreeing that the fruit's true home was in the south of the continent. But it was not until 2014 that genetic research in Munich showed conclusively that watermelon is native to western Africa.

Watermelon and its close relatives, the tsamma and the bitter colocynth – all members of *Citrullus* – have been growing wild in the wastes of western, central and southern Africa for millennia. There, Bushmen and other tribes adopted the juicy fruit, which served not only as a food but as a valuable source of water. Even today it is a central part of nomadic Bushmen life. Eventually watermelon or its seeds were carried

Watermelons growing wild in the Western Desert, Egypt.

to North Africa, where some believe it was domesticated. The oldest watermelon seeds yet found come from Egypt, dating back 6,000 years, while 5,000-year-old seeds have been excavated in Libya and 5,000-year-old watermelon rind has been found in South Africa. Seeds and leaves were reported from the Egyptian 12th Dynasty (2000–1800 BC) and seeds were found in King Tutankhamun's tomb (c. 1325 BC).

From the north of Africa, watermelon travelled into India and on into Asia. Some believe this dramatic geographic spread happened very early, as early as the second or first millennium BC; others claim that it didn't occur until far later, in around AD 800. The historian J. R. McNeill suggests that crops such as sorghum, millet and watermelon travelled from

A colocynth plant in an Ottoman-era copy (*c.* 1700) of a medieval manuscript (*c.* 1250).

Africa to India in the second and first millennium BC, during what he calls the 'Monsoon Exchange'. Recent linguistic evidence in Sanskrit and Persian suggests that trade in watermelon was taking place between the two peoples as early as the sixth century BC, when northwest India came under Persian control.

Sweet melons – and other *Cucumis melo* fruits – are much harder to identify in the archaeological record than watermelons. Sweet melons' thin rinds almost never survive and the seeds of one *C. melo* variety are pretty much indistinguishable not only from the seeds of every other variety of sweet melon but from cucumber seeds as well, without the aid of a genetics laboratory. Still, many scientists and historians were almost certain that sweet melons originated in Africa. But in 2010 the botanists Susanne Renner and others at the University of Munich published the results of their DNA research, which showed unequivocally that *Cucumis melo* – sweet melons – originated in the Indian subcontinent and probably the lowlands of the Himalayas.

The earliest sweet melon remains to have been discovered in India date to between 2300 and 1600 BC in the Indus Valley and to around 1600 BC in western central India. The aboriginal inhabitants of India – called the Munda – had many words for various types of *C. melo* melons (and none for watermelon or its relatives). As the Sanskrit-speaking Indo-Aryans moved into India in the second and first millennium BC, they adopted some Munda words for melons, including *carbhatah* or *cirbhita* – the root of the Latin *cucurbit*. A Sanskrit Ayurvedic name for the netted melon (that is, muskmelon) appears to have Munda roots as well, making the name some 4,000 years old.

Sweet melons must have spread very early from India to Iran. A large quantity of melon seeds dating back to 3000 BC has been found in the mysterious 'Burnt City' Shahr-i-Shōkhta – one of the first cities in human history, in southeastern Iran – but whether these seeds are from sweet melons or green vegetable melons is unclear. Considering that scientists believe Iran to be one of the primary centres of diversification of the sweet melon, there is surprisingly little data on melons in ancient Persia. Despite that lack of information, the Persian language indicates an intimate and long-standing acquaint - ance with the fruit and contains many terms either for melons themselves or for describing melons, such as sweet melon, small yet odorous melon, sour melon, unripe melon, soft/ rotten melon, a place where melons grow and so on. The Persian word for melon, *kharbuz* or *kharbuza* (meaning 'large cucumber/cucurbit') – which was very likely a loan word from the Munda/Sanskrit *carbhatah* – was then re-adopted in its new form into the Sanskrit language when the Persians invaded India in the fifth century BC. One of the Hindi words for melon is still *kharbuz*, but most modern descendants of the Persian *kharbuz* – including the Turkish *karpuz*, the Greek *karpouzi*, the Russian *arpuz* and the Sanskrit *kharbuja* – refer to the watermelon rather than the sweet melon.

When exactly sweet melons reached China from India is unclear. Melon seeds have been uncovered in Zhejiang dating back to 3000 BC and in Shaanxi to 2000 BC, although there is a good chance these seeds were the conomon melon. Perhaps sweet melons as well as jade and gold were acquired by the Chinese in their earliest forays west: according to the botanist Terrence W. Walters, muskmelon and pickling melon were 'the most important fruit-vegetables' during the Western Zhou dynasty (1100–771 BC). We do know that melons were common by the time of the Han dynasty in China (206 BC–AD 220) – a recent autopsy of the mummified remains of a woman from the Han showed that her stomach was full of melon seeds. (Melon seeds are still a popular snack throughout Asia and the Near and Middle East). The Marquis of Eastern Mound reportedly lost his wealth in the Han period but was able to support himself by raising what were said to be very good melons.

In Arabia and the Mediterranean the melon's history is a bit tangled. Melon seeds have been reported in eastern Arabia that have been dated to 2900 BC but, again, whether these remains are of sweet or vegetable melons – or even cucumbers – is still unknown. In Mesopotamia (now Iraq) lies the land once known as Sumer, which had a language unrelated to any other known language and what seems to be the first written language in history. There it has been said that the great Sumerian law-giver Ur-Nammu of Ur grew melons and cucumbers in his fabled gardens. There is indeed evidence that Ur-Nammu – who founded the Sumerian 3rd Dynasty of Ur in southern Mesopotamia around 2047–2030 BC and built the Great Ziggurat of Ur – was familiar with some types of cucurbit, and that those were probably members of *Cucumis*. But were these ancient cucurbits sweet melons, vege - table melons or cucumbers? The arguments are complex and ongoing.

Water dropper in the form of a melon, Korea, 12th century.

This clay tablet with cuneiform inscription gives a list of plants
in the garden of Merodach-Baladan. The fourth column contains
a figure that is translated as melon.

One way to unravel what Ur-Nammu was eating in the
way of melons is to take a look at what he was saying in his
native Sumerian language. Ancient Sumerian has a word,
ukuš, which became the ancient Semitic Akkadian *qiššu* that
is usually translated as 'cucumber'. (A quick historical note:
the Akkadians were the successors to the Sumerians and the
predecessors of the Babylonians and Assyrians. Unlike the
mysterious Sumerian language, Akkadian is related to Hebrew

and Arabic.) Of this so-called *ukuš* or *qiššu* 'cucumber', both 'summer' and 'winter' kinds were known, as well as 'ripe', 'sweet' and 'bitter'. If you've ever grown cucumbers yourself, you know that 'ripe' or 'sweet' are not words normally associated with cucumbers. If you (or an ancient Sumerian) were growing melons rather than cucumbers, wouldn't descriptors like 'ripe' and 'sweet' make much more sense? This leads to speculation that, indeed, *ukuš* and *qiššu* actually indicated a type of melon and that melons were grown and relished in ancient Sumer and Akkad and, of course, later Babylonia and Israel. Ten seeds of an unidentified cucurbit from an Old Akkadian site (2500–1950 BC) at Tell Taya near Mosul in modern Iraq have been discovered but until scientists can positively identify those seeds in a laboratory, it seems likely that we will not know exactly what kinds of melons Sumerians were eating.

In seventh-century BC Mesopotamia, the Babylonian king Merodach-Baladan II was a noted gardener who was reputed to have grown delicious melons. Merodach-Baladan's plant list shows us that he grew colocynths (the bitter 'watermelon') but it is unlikely that anyone would consider this a delicious melon! The other cucurbit in his plant list can be translated as melon, cucumber or gourd. One tantalizing clue, however, comes from a depiction of a scene from an Assyrian banquet dating to the time of Ashurbanipal (685 BC–*c*. 627 BC). On the table in front of the guests there are various fruits, including what appears to be a nice, neat slice of melon.

What about sweet melons in Egypt? There are references to melons or some type of cucurbit, usually cucumber, in ancient stories – but these references can confuse as well as illuminate. One of the earliest is in the oldest 'Robinson Crusoe' story in history, the Egyptian *Tale of the Shipwrecked Sailor*, which dates to about 2200 BC. It is the story of a man on his way to

37

work in the mines of the Pharaoh when he is shipwrecked as he approaches Egypt. As he struggles ashore at last, hungry and thirsty, he describes what happened next: 'I laid me in a thicket . . .Then I stretched my limbs to try to find something for my mouth. I found there figs and grain, melons, fishes and birds.' A similar clue comes from the Hebrew Bible, in Numbers 11:5, when the ancient Israelites wander in the desert, lamenting the life they had known in Egypt: 'We remember the fish, which we did eat in Egypt freely; the cucumbers, and the melons, and the leeks, and the onions, and the garlic. But now our soul is dried away . . .'. In these two accounts, separated by centuries, we seem to learn that Egyptians ate melons and cucumbers. But did they?

The cucurbit researcher Harry S. Paris and his colleagues David C. Parrish and J. Janick have argued convincingly that there were no true cucumbers in the ancient Mediterranean and that references to 'cucumbers' – whether in Hebrew, Egyptian, Roman, Greek or possibly even Sumerian and Assyrian sources – actually refer to chate and snake melons. These researchers base this on a number of clues: first, that the visual depictions of 'cucumbers' – in tile, in sculpture and

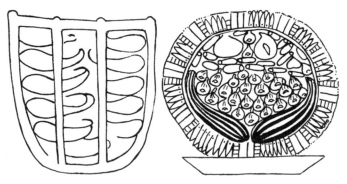

Images from tombs in Thebes, Egypt, c. 1400 BC: chate melons on the left and snake melons on the right.

Young watermelon showing distinctive hairs or 'fuzz'.

in paintings – in ancient sites around the Mediterranean don't show cucumbers but rather seem to show the snake melons and immature fruits of chate melons. The key here, oddly enough, is fuzz. One of the things that distinguishes young chate melons from cucumbers is that the immature chate fruit is covered with fine, soft hairs which must be removed before eating. So marked is this fuzz or hair that methods for removing it are described in early Hebrew manuscripts. Importantly this hairy fuzz also occurs on other types of melons but *not* on cucumbers – yet this fuzz shows clearly in many ancient illustrations of so-called 'cucumbers' and is described in the written record as well. Other written descriptions of 'cucumbers' in the ancient world describe a long, coiled, serpent-like fruit, which sounds very much like the snake melon. The ancient Hebrew word for these young chate melons (and sometimes,

[Cucurbita citrullus.]

ABATTACHIM (אֲבַטִּחִים ; Sept. σίκυος).

The biblical *abattachim* (melon).

as well, the snake melons) was *kishu* (plural *kishuim*), which is obviously very closely related to the Semitic Akkadian *qiššu*, from the Sumerian *ukuš*. All of these are related to the later Arabic *qitha* or *qatta*, which became, in modern English, 'chate'. Chates have been growing wild in tropical Africa and the Nile delta for thousands of years. According to the *Encyclopedia of Jewish Food*, chate melons were being preserved in salt 4,000 years ago in Egypt and Mesopotamia.

So if in ancient Egypt 'cucumbers' were actually chate or snake melons, what are the 'melons' described by the Egyptian sailor and the Israelites? Most scholars now believe that sweet melons, such as cantaloupe, were not introduced into Egypt until the common era. The Hebrew word used in the Israelites' lament indicates that the longed-for melon was actually a watermelon, which accords well with the evidence that watermelons were common in Egypt by the time of the Hebrew Bible. In the case of the shipwrecked sailor, the hieroglyph used in his story suggests that the luscious fruit that slaked the sailor's hunger and thirst was a cultivated melon – definitely not a watermelon, possibly a chate.

Chate melons were called the 'Egyptian melon', according to the Swedish explorer and naturalist Fredrik Hasselquist. (They were also known as the 'queen of cucumbers', just to keep the confusion going.) Today, chate melons are often described as bland and insipid. But Hasselquist disagreed. In 1749 he wrote:

> This fruit is a little watery, the flesh is almost of the same substance as the Melons, it tastes somewhat sweet and cool, but is far from being as cool as the Water Melone. This the grandees and Europeans in Egypt eat as the most pleasant fruit they find . . . It is the most excellent fruit of this tribe, of any yet known. The Princes and grandees in Europe may wish they could get it into their gardens, for it is certainly worth a place on their tables.

3

The Melon in the Classical Period

If you're fond of esoteric yet very heated arguments, try getting into a debate with linguists, culinary historians and botanists about whether or not the Greeks and the Romans ate melons – or, at least, melons as we now know them. For it is in the classical period that the naming of cucurbits and melons goes from merely confusing to total chaos. As usual, the ancient Greeks started it.

The Greeks called the 'cucumber' – which, as in Egypt, was probably a young chate melon or a snake melon – *sikyos* (related to the Sumerian *ukuš*). Although numerous *C. melo* seeds (variety unknown) have been uncovered in seventh-century BC Samos, in Greece, it wasn't until the fourth century BC that Hippocrates, the father of Western medicine, talked about a cucurbit he called a *sikyos pepon*. *Pepon* means 'soft' or 'ripe', so *sikyos pepon* would be a 'ripe cucumber'. This *sikyos pepon* soon became known simply as *pepon*. But what exactly was this 'ripe cucumber'?

Many scholars are fairly convinced that there were no actual cucumbers in ancient Greece and that the *sikyos pepon* was indeed a melon. As to what type, arguments abound, but many agree with the scholar Alfred C. Andrews, whose investigations of the classical literature in the 1950s labelled the *pepon* or *sikyos pepon* as the watermelon. Andrews especially cites Aristotle's claim that the *sikyos pepon* grew very well in Egypt. The earlier Old Comedic writer Cratinus also wrote of a 'huge *sikyos* full of seeds' – which does indeed sound like a watermelon. Recent archaeological finds in Platamona, Greece, include an amphora containing watermelon seeds that date back to the second millennium BC. It should not be surprising that the Greeks knew of watermelon, given the amount of contact between the Greeks and the Egyptians, for whom watermelon was common. Yet it is odd that the Greeks don't mention this *pepon* very often and don't talk about its wonderful sweetness, which is often present even in wild watermelons.

By the second century of the modern era Greek physicians such as Galen were talking about the *melopepon*, *melo* meaning apple-like or round – so, a 'round melon'. A round melon or cucurbit would have been a contrast to the elongate cucurbits the Greeks had been familiar with, but so far no one has discovered exactly what this round melon was.

Abraham Brueghel, *Ceres at a Fountain, Attended by Putti*, 1665–75. The cherubic putti are feasting on watermelon.

The Romans called their cucumber-like fruits *cucumis* or *cucumers* instead of the Greek *sikyos*, but they adopted the Greeks' *melopepon* and *pepo* – the latter usually indicating a large curcubit. (Our English word 'pumpkin' comes from *pepo* and, of course, 'melon' comes from *melo*.) The antiquarian physician Ludovicus Nonnius mentions that *melopepones* were a superior species of *pepones*. Whether he was referring to watermelons we don't know, but there are depictions of watermelon in Roman art by the end of the first century AD. The Romans also used *cucurbita*, which seems to mostly refer to gourd-like fruits – although, typically, there is some argument about this. In the first century AD the scientist and historian Pliny the Elder refers to large *cucumers* as *pepones* which, again, sound very much as though they could be watermelons. Pliny's son wrote about watermelons he had seen in Egypt, calling them all 'colocynth', although it seems clear from his descriptions and context that some of the melons he had seen were citron melons and some sweet watermelons, though others were indeed the bitter medicinal colocynth.

But it was Pliny the Elder's description of a new type of cucurbit that might be the most interesting:

Curious to say, just recently a new form of cucumber has been produced in Campania, shaped like a quince. I am told that first one grew in this shape by accident, and that later a variety was established grown from seed obtained from this one; it is called apple pumpkin (*melopepo*). Cucumbers of this kind do not hang from the plant but grow of a round shape lying on the ground; they have a golden colour. A remarkable thing about them, beside their shape, colour and smell, is that when they have ripened, although they are not hanging down they at once separate from the stalk when ripe.

Pliny's description could not be clearer – his new quince-shaped (or apple-shaped) 'cucumber' was very likely a sweet melon, and very likely a type of muskmelon or cantaloupe: it was round, it grew lying on the ground, it had an odour, it was golden in colour and, most importantly, it separated from the stalk when ripe – something which very few other cucurbits except *C. melo* do. Although arguments about when sweet melons were introduced into the Roman world continue, it seems that Pliny regarded the round, golden melon as a startling new development. Perhaps Galen's *melopepon* was a similar melon.

The emperor Tiberius (42 BC–AD 37) was said to be so fond of eating melons (some stories say cucumbers) that he had special greenhouses built so that he could have them every day. It is true that the first known greenhouses, probably using mica instead of glass, were built for Tiberius' pleasure, and it is also true that Tiberius had a curcurbit of some sort on his table nearly every day but, according to the researchers Harry S Paris and his colleagues David C. Parrish and J. Janick, the melons/cucumbers that Tiberius ate were very probably gourds that were eaten like courgettes (zucchini) when young. It is also possible that they were the snake melons that Columella (*c*. AD 4–70) described in his popular treatise on Roman agriculture, *De re rustica* (in which no sweet melons are described):

> . . . and the twisted cucumber (*cucumis*)
> And swelling gourd (*cucurbita*), sometimes from arbours
>   hang,
> Sometimes, like snakes beneath the summer sun,
> Through the cool shadow of the grass do creep.

It is frequently reported that the Romans spread the cultivation of melons – which kind is not usually specified – to the farthest reaches of their empire where growing conditions were favourable. Yet neither sweet melons nor watermelons are mentioned very often in classical literature. The eighteenth-century botanist Alphonse de Candolle says of melon in the classical period: 'It was probably of indifferent quality, to judge from the silence or the faint praise of writers in a country where gourmets were not wanting.'

4

Melons in Late Antiquity and the Medieval Period

There shall you admire vineyards as fecund in abundant foliage
as they are magnificent in generous and joyful fruit. There shall
you see gardens to be commended for the admirable variety of
their fruits . . . whence the waters flow in rivulets to every place,
to irrigate the gardens, to restore and nourish the cucumbers,
small and short, the longer squashes, the melons which grow
almost to a sphere

Hugo Falcandus describing gardens in Sicily in *Praefatio ad Petrum*, *c.* 1190

Many scholars believe that it wasn't until the end of the
medieval period, in the late 1400s, that truly sweet and delicious melons were introduced into Italy from Armenia and
that from there sweet melons spread into the rest of Europe.
Yet there is certainly evidence to suggest that at least some
Europeans knew about and sometimes grew sweet melons –
and watermelons – before 1400.

In AD 388 the Roman Augustine of Hippo mocked the
Persian followers of Mani for their veneration of melons,
saying,

> Why do you look upon a yellow melon as part of the
> treasures of God, and not rancid bacon fat or the yolk of

47

an egg? . . . Indeed, you sometimes go so far as to say that an usurer is more harmless than a cultivator, you feel so much more for melons than for men. Rather than hurt the melons, you would have a man ruined as a debtor.

Whether Augustine had eaten yellow melons or not, we don't know, but he did not feel it necessary to explain what these yellow melons were to his readers in the Christian West.

The Roman Palladius, also writing in the fourth century, gave directions to grow 'Melons to sette in Marche and make hem sweete as Mylke and smellynge as rosis', advising gardeners: 'Now sow melon seed two feet apart in prepared ground, but steep the seed three days in milk or mead, and set them when dry. Keep the melons in rose-leaves to make them odorous.' (Twelve hundred years later, St Francis de Sales would give similar directions for ensuring melons would be sweet by soaking the seeds before planting in musk or sugar.)

Melons figure in the famous Roman cookbook attributed to Apicius, known as the *De re coquinaria* (On Cookery). The book dates to the fifth century and has recipes for '*pepones et melones*' – which certainly sound like what we have been told should be watermelons and melons. But the recipes are mostly for a salad that dresses the *pepones* or *melones* with pepper, pennyroyal (a kind of mint) and a mix of vinegar, broth and various herbs. One recipe concludes that 'sometimes one adds silphium' (an extinct pungent herb).

Apicius' recipe is very similar to one described by Anthimus (AD 511–534), a Greek Byzantine physician at the court of the 'barbarian' king of the Romans, Theodoric the Great. In his cookbook, *De observatione ciborum* (On the Observance of Foods), Anthimus says of *melones*: 'If melons are well ripened, their flesh is particularly recommended mixed with their own seeds . . . If, as people do, they are eaten like this with diluted vinegar (*posca*) and a sprinkling of pennyroyal, they are good for healthy people.' It is entirely possible that these *melones* dressed with vinegar and herbs were our sweet melons – after all, many people still eat some types of melon with salt and pepper. Yet it is interesting that Anthimus puts *melones* in his list of vegetables such as radishes and onions and not in his list of fruits alongside sweet grapes, peaches and apples. One modern scholar believes that Anthimus' *melones* were actually watermelon. Certainly the popular modern Greek recipe for watermelon salad dressed with aged vinegar and mint, along with feta cheese, sounds quite similar to Anthimus' ancient recipe.

Melons also figured in the capitularies, or edicts, of the great king of the Franks and emperor of the Romans Charlemagne in AD 800. One capitulary, which recommended food plants to be grown in the gardens of the empire, included four cucurbits: *cucumeres* (cucumbers), *cucurbitas* (gourds), *coloquentidas* (colocynths, the bitter medicinal watermelon relatives) and *pepones*. *Pepones* is often translated as 'pumpkin' – which we know is not right since there were no pumpkins in Europe before Columbus – but no one is quite sure whether it referred to sweet melons or watermelons, nor how good those were.

Another tantalizing reference to sweet melons is given by Walafrid Strabo (*c.* 808–849), the abbot of the Benedictine monastery at Reichenau in southern Germany. Strabo was a poet and gardener as well as a monk, and one of his most important works was his charming book *Hortulus* (The Little Garden). In it he describes what sounds very much like a European cantaloupe:

> When a knife blade finds the guts of a melon a gush of juice comes out and many seeds with it. Then your lucky guest can divide by hand the hollow body into several

49

Calissons, a Provençal sweet made primarily of melon paste, sugar and ground almonds, may have roots in medieval Italy and Venice.

pieces and thus enjoy the luscious delicacy. Its freshness and savour delight the palate; nor can this food defeat a man's teeth, for it's easy to eat and its natural properties cool and refresh his whole inner body.

In Spain documents from fifth-century Navarre indicate that melons were used as church offerings, although we don't know what kind. However, after the Moorish conquest of Spain in the 700s we find numerous written citations of melons.

The invading Moors – North African and Arab Muslims – brought many varieties of melon and watermelon to the Iberian Peninsula. When exactly the Arabs learned of sweet melon is unknown, but it is likely that their trading contacts in Persia and the Near East introduced them very early to the fruit and its cultivation. They certainly knew the watermelon by the Islamic age. In 961 the Mozarabic cleric Rabi ibn Zaid (Recemundus) presented an Arabic calendar of Christian holidays to the new caliph of Al-Andalus in Spain, al-Hakim II. This 'Calendar of Cordoba' contained gardening information, including dates when melons and watermelons should be planted and harvested:

> April is the month when 'small melons' are sown.
> June is the month when the first sweet melons appear.
> August is the month when . . . the watermelons, known as 'al-hindi', are now ripe.

The plants lists of Moorish royal gardener Ibn Bassal, c. 1080, included both melon and watermelon. Abu al-Khayr of Seville, writing around 1100, listed a number of melons, including one he called 'sugary' and another he dubbed 'Armini'

Watermelon-feta salad. The recipe may have roots in the ancient world.

(Armenian), which had a smooth yellow skin, a sweet taste and a pleasant aroma. One hundred years later, Ibn al-'Awwam of Seville wrote the *Kitab al-filaha*, the most important Muslim work on agriculture and gardening and the most important medieval one on the subject. The plant list of the *Kitab* mentioned watermelon, 'two sorts', as well as a number of sweet melon types, one of which sounds very much like a casaba melon – the kind of melon still most popular in Spain today. A poem about a jilted lover from medieval Moorish Spain also references a melon with similarities to the casaba:

> When I sent you my melons, you cried out with scorn,
> They ought to be heavy and wrinkled and yellow;
> When I offered myself, whom those graces adorn,
> You flouted, and called me an ugly old fellow.

Melons were now appearing in written records on the outskirts of Europe. Hungarian records show that sweet melons were being cultivated in the early eleventh century and Hungarians were eating watermelon by the twelfth century, judging from the seeds that archaeologists have found in medieval sites.

In the Byzantine capital of Constantinople, Simeon Seth, a Jewish Greek doctor and scholar, reported that new varieties of fruits were arriving from the East, including the 'so-called Saracen melon'. To Seth, 'Saracen' generally meant any Muslim, with no indication of ethnicity, but what type of melon or watermelon Seth was talking about, we don't know. 'Arab traders' and 'Saracens' – who may have been Kurds and Seljuk Turks – were credited with bringing sesame, carob, millet, rice, lemons, melons, apricots and shallots to Europe during the Ayyubid Dynasty, centred in Cairo during the twelfth and thirteenth centuries.

Watermelon (*battikh*) plant, illustrated in a medieval Arabic manuscript.

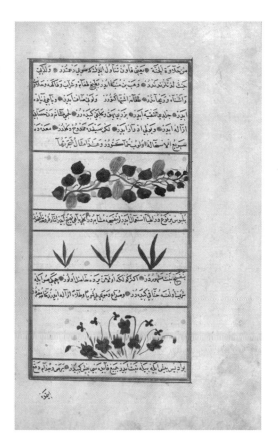

In 1200 the Orthodox Christian monk Anthony of Novgorod in Russia travelled to Constantinople:

> In the precinct of St Sophia there are wells, and the Patriarch's garden and many chapels. All kinds of fruit for the Patriarch: melons, apples, and pears, are kept there in a well: they are placed in a basket on the end of a long rope, and when the Patriarch is to eat they pull them out, quite chilled. The Emperor eats in this way too.

Albertus Magnus (*c.* 1200–1280), the Dominican monk and teacher of Thomas Aquinas, is often credited with the first reports of watermelons in Europe. As we have seen, the Moorish gardeners in Spain wrote about watermelons more than 200 years before Albert the Great, although watermelons were certainly not common in medieval Europe. But Albert the Great's works give us some idea of the confusion surrounding melon/cucurbit identification in older records. To quote the nineteenth-century American botanist Edward Sturtevant:

> Albertus Magnus, in the thirteenth century, says, melons, which some call pepones, have the seed and the flower

'Anguria' or watermelon, from the *Carrara Herbal* (1390–1404), attributed to Serapion the Younger.

very nearly like those of the cucumber and also says, in speaking of the cucumber, that the seeds are like those of the pepo. Under the head of watermelon, citrullus, he calls the melon pepo, and says it has a smooth, green skin, but the pepo is commonly yellow and of an uneven surface and as if round, semi-circular sections were orderly arranged together.

As difficult as that description is to untangle, it seems clear that the 'pepo' in the last sentence was a European cantaloupe type, with a golden knobbly skin divided into natural segments.

By the fourteenth century sweet melons were becoming increasingly common. In the early 1300s Simon Fitzsimmons, an Irish Franciscan monk, travelled from Ireland to Jerusalem and described a shipside scene in Heraklion, in Crete: 'This city . . . abounds . . . in fruit . . .The ships and galleys were loaded with cheese and that famous Cretan wine . . . Pomegran - ates, lemons, figs, grapes, melons, watermelons, gourds and other kinds of fruits could be purchased at the smallest price.' Giovanni Villani (*c.* 1280–1348) tells us in his *Chronicles* that 4,000 loads of melons entered the city of Florence through one gate in July of 1338 – and also assures us that this was a normal annual total. And then there are the spectacular medieval manuscripts known as the *Tacuinum sanitatis*, with their stunning visual images of all types of melons in all their fecund glory. These were beautifully illustrated Latin versions of an eleventh-century Arabic gardening manuscript, produced at the end of the 1300s in Italy. Each of these manuscripts contains over 200 full-page detailed coloured illustrations of garden plants – including leaf, flower and fruit.

There are a quite a few kinds of cucurbit depicted in the *Tacuinum*. The researchers Harry S. Paris, David C. Parrish and J. Janick have identified chate melons (labelled as *Cucumeres*

'Melones dulces' – sweet watermelons – from the Vienna *Tacuinum sanitatis* (*c.* 1390).

& cetruli), what appears to be a casaba melon (also labelled as *Cucumeres & cetruli*, possibly indicating that it was eaten as a 'cucumber' when immature) and snake melons (labelled *Langurie*). One picture, labelled in some versions as *Melones indi i palestini*, shows a man holding a round, yellow melon to his nose, indicating fragrance – doesn't that sound like a musk - melon or cantaloupe? There are also clear illustrations of the watermelon, labelled *Melones dulces* – and the recommendation they be eaten with ripe cheese, salty foods and fine wine – and

of the preserving 'citron' melon, labelled *Melones insipidi*. In addition there are images of oval, yellow-green melons that are described as 'sweet and watery', which are also labelled *Melones insipidi*. Paris and his co-workers identify this 'insipid melon' as an early ancestor of the cantaloupe and speculate that the sweetness we so identify with our modern melons was still not fully developed in the fourteenth century. Perhaps this explains Bartholomeus the Englishman's lament in 1398, 'Suche werische [insipid] things ben melones.'

Looking at the historical record, it seems that sweet melons in Europe during the medieval period were known and sometimes – if grown under the right conditions – could be sweet and delicious. But if the wrong seed were chosen or growing conditions weren't optimal, the melons could be bland and somewhat tasteless – a complaint of melon growers to this day.

5
Melons on the Silk Road

Grapes of Turfan are the best, sweet melons of Shanshan are
the sweetest, and the lamb of Kucha is like a flower.
Saying in Xinxiang, China, along the Silk Road

Melon cultivation has been carried by the Kumulik to a fine
art. On a sandy or stony patch the plants are so trained as to
allow each fruit to rest upon a dry, sand-baked spot, where
it absorbs the heat of the torrid rays. The grower must work
ceaselessly in his garden . . . and when the fruit has come
to perfection he and his assistant never leave the tiny lodge
from which they watch their precious merchandise, even
taking it in turn to sleep.
Mildred Cable and Francesca French,
Through Jade Gate and Central Asia (1927)

Europeans and Englishmen may have had to suffer insipid
melons before the modern era, but that was not the case in
the Near East, in Central Asia and along the famous Silk Road,
where some of the world's best melons were and still are
grown in the lush oases. It makes sense that some of the
world's best melons would grow along this famous trade route
– the irrigated oases under hot desert sun made for optimal

growing conditions and traders provided both a market for the best melons and a means of distributing the best seeds.

Stretching nearly 5,000 miles across China, Central Asia and the Near East to the Mediterranean Sea, the Silk Road was one of the greatest trade routes the world has ever known. Chinese princes hungry for jade, horses and glass sent their traders west, while Roman and Byzantine princes desirous of silks, jewels and spices sent their traders east, and soldiers, refugees and monks went both ways. For nearly 2,000 years travellers, monks, traders, tribes and armies participated in this enormous cross-cultural fertilization across a huge expanse stretching from Constantinople to Chang'an, bringing with them not only silks and jewels but their technologies, culture,

Melon vendor in Samarkand.

ideas and religions. Death, too, travelled the Road: the plague was brought from Asia to Europe over this route. More happily, flowers, vegetables and fruits were carried as well: roses, chrysanthemums, peonies and oranges went west; grapes, figs, cucumbers, walnut and sesame went east. And then there were the delicious melons that would become famous in the cities and oases along the Silk Road.

In virtually all of the central cities of the Silk Road, from Merv, Maru, Samarkand, Bukhara, Bactra and Tashkent, to the harsh steppes of Central Asia and in the oases of Khotan, Khwarezm, Shan-shan, Kucha, Turfan and Hami, melons were grown and known for their sweetness. In the thriving and exotic Silk Road Persian city of Merv under the Seljuk Turks, special pigeonhouses were built. The pigeons were used in delicately spiced dishes, and their droppings were used to fertilize the succulent melons for which Merv was famous. Pigeonhouses built to harvest the droppings for melons still

Ancient pigeon towers, which still dot the landscape in Iran. Pigeon dung was collected as fertilizer for crops, especially melons.

dot the landscape at Isfahan. And at both ends of the road –
Baghdad and Aleppo in the West and the ancient Chinese
capitals of Chang'an and Loyang in the East – melons were
a prominent feature of daily life.

In the 900s Al-Warraq, the compiler of the first Arabic
cookbook yet discovered, cites the many kinds of melons
available in Baghdad and throughout the Abbasid Caliphate.
There was the 'Chinese' melon with a rough skin, described
as 'sweet as honey, aromatic as musk, and enclosed in a vest
of gold'. (This sounds very much like a muskmelon or cantaloupe type.) There was the Khurasan melon, which had a twisted
neck and was not as sweet. There was the small, round *shimmam*
melon, apparently common in Iraq and Lebanon, with a red
and yellow striped rind and a gorgeously sweet smell. There
was a variety of watermelon, 'the sweetest and nicest-tasting
of all melons', which was grown at Maru in Persia and also
in Khwarezm. This watermelon was exported from Khwarezm
to Baghdad, packed inside lead containers full of ice, as early
as the reign of the Abassid caliph al-Ma'mun (813–833). Other
types of melons were also listed, including non-sweet types
that sound like snake melons, and watermelons – not as
good, apparently, as the Khwarezm watermelons, but nevertheless described as 'like an oval box made of ivory, striped
with emerald, with a ruby hiding inside'.

Al-Warraq's Baghdad cookbook included a number of
recipes with melon as a main ingredient. One called for the
sweetest melon you could find, pared so as to get only the
sweetest part of the flesh. The melon flesh was cooked alone
until most of the water was boiled away, and then honey and
eggs were added. This pudding was baked under a roasting
chicken, so as to absorb the drippings, then served alongside
the chicken. Another pudding, also using the sweetest melon
available, called for pared melon pulp to be sweetened with

honey, scented with saffron and thickened with starch – it was
sometimes sweetened again with a bit of sugar if the honey
and melon were not sufficient.

The famous Islamic Kurdish scholar and traveller Ibn
Hawqal, in 955, described 'long' and 'ugly' melons grown in
Persia that were 'infinitely sweet, very good to eat'. So good
were these Persian melons, according to Ibn Hawqal, that they
were nearly as delicious as the 'renowned melons of Khorasan'.

Painting of Abdulla Khan Uzbek II slicing melons, *c.* 1590.

Sicilian watermelon pudding, with pistachios and jasmine hinting at its 'Arabian Nights' origins.

In China melon growing was an important enterprise. A book written by Chia Ssu-hsieh in the sixth century contained an entire chapter devoted to the culture of melons, including methods of obtaining good seeds for reproduction, breeding for fungal resistance, the selection of fruit shapes and sizes and the methods of planting. Along with information on musk - melons the book gave facts on the growing of pickling melon, cucumber, winter melon and bottle gourd.

Melons also figure in the wanderings of some of the great peripatetic Buddhist scholars and monks, including the great seventh-century Buddhist monk Xuanzang (*c.* 602–664), who travelled from China to India hoping to discover the original

Sanskrit documents of Buddhism. Following the Silk Road west through the fearsome Taklamakan desert (the name translates roughly as 'he goes in but doesn't come out'), Xuanzang came to Turfan, where the king outfitted him with equipment and servants and provided a caravan laden down with gold, silver, hundreds of rolls of silk and luscious grapes and melons, destined not only for Xuanzang's use but for kings along the way, including the Grand Khan of the Turks. In India Xuanzang described the edible herbs and plants he encountered there, such as ginger, mustard, gourds and, notably, melons.

It is clear from such travellers' tales that melons were an expected delicacy on the arduous Silk Road. But they were also a staple in the cities and royal courts. Xuanzang was the Tang Dynasty's (618–906) most famous monk, but the Tang period was also known for the sophisticated court life that the nobles enjoyed, which included delicious melons. The poet Li Shangyin (c. 813–858) lamented his lost love,

> The fine melon stretches its long tendrils;
> Its green jade freezes in the cold water.
> Though its five colours shine at Eastern Mound
> How can one bear to bite its fragrant flesh?

The emperors' palace contained a 'cool hall' that was air-conditioned by water-powered fans and fountains, and there were ice pits in the parks outside the palace where melons could be kept properly chilled in summer.

From 947 to 953 Hu Kiao of China travelled in the northern country of the Mongol tribe the Kitan (Marco Polo's 'Cathay'), where he saw watermelon for the first time. The Kitan told Hu Kiao that they had received the seed from a Central Asian Turkic tribe, the Uighurs. Hu Kiao says, 'They cultivated the plant by covering the seeds with cattle-manure and placing mats over the beds. The fruit is as large as that of the tun kwa [a type of wax gourd] and of sweet taste.'

There are some reports that watermelons from Khwarezm were imported – packed in ice inside lead containers – to the Chinese imperial capital in the ninth century. Even if watermelons were imported that early, they may have been strictly a novelty. Hun Hao (1109–1155), who was the Chinese ambassador to Jurchen (now Manchuria), says in his memoirs: 'The watermelon (si kwa or western melon) . . . is very green in colour, almost blue-green . . . This Cucurbitacea resembles the sweet melon and is sweet and crisp. Its interior is filled with a juice that is very cold.' Hun Hao brought seeds back to China: 'At present it is found both in the imperial orchards and in village gardens. It can be kept for several months, aside from the fact that there is nothing to prevent it from assuming a yellow hue in course of time.' Reportedly the Jurchens learned of the watermelon from the Kitan, 'western melon' being a melon from the west of China, that is, Central Asia. By the end of the thirteenth century watermelons were eaten regularly in China. A charming rural poem from that period describes a picnic where little watermelons were gulped down, seeds and all.

In 1206 the fearsome Genghis (or Chingis) Khan rose as ruler of all the Mongols. He invaded most of Asia and created an empire that stretched from eastern Europe to the Sea of Japan, the largest contiguous empire in the history of the world, encompassing over 100 million people. In 1221 the Daoist monk Qiu Chuji was summoned to appear before Genghis and travelled from Shanghai to Central Asia, through Samar - kand, then over the Hindu Kush to Afghanistan where Genghis was holding court. As we might expect, Qiu Chuji reportedly noted with surprise and delight the flavour, sweetness and size of the Central Asian melons that he ate along the way.

Genghis Khan's 'Mongol Peace' brought a period of calm and safety to the long Silk Road, governed as it now was by one empire. That peace encouraged more travellers, one of whom was Marco Polo – and Marco was enchanted by the melons he found on his journey.

In 1271 Marco, with his father, Maffeo, and uncle Nicolo, set off from Italy on a mission to China to see Kubilai Khan, Genghis Khan's grandson. They joined the Silk Road near Balkh in what is now northern Afghanistan after passing through a desert of 'surpassing aridity'. Marco described the experience:

> in these deserts you find no water, but have to carry it with you. The beasts do without drink until you have got across the desert tract and come to watering places . . . So after travelling for six days as I have told you, you come to a city called Sapurgan [west of Balkh]. It has great plenty of everything, but especially of the very best melons in the world. They preserve them by paring them round and round into strips, and drying them in the sun. When dry they are sweeter than honey, and are carried off for sale all over the country.

Both Persia and Afghanistan, where Marco Polo saw melons being preserved, were quite well known for their melons by the thirteenth century. The great Persian epic poet Hamd Allah Qazvini (also called Hamdollah Mostowfi, 1281–1349) says that melons were grown in 'every garden' in Iran and there were many varieties. One Muslim elder of Herat (in what is now Afghanistan) was said to have 50 kinds in his garden alone, and the finest melons were also grown for export in ten Iranian cities, including Tabriz and the Silk Road cities of Isfahan and Merv. Watermelon, however, was only

This illuminated manuscript shows Sheikh Mahneh of Khorasan (967–1049) and a villager, with men weighing melons in the background, 1487.

Chinese painting from the 17th century showing mice nibbling a melon, a fruit considered lucky because of the many seeds, which symbolize having many children.

mentioned by Hamd Allah as growing in the city of Qazvin (north of Tehran). In addition to eating melons straight from the garden, Persian cooks made delicious drinks such as the iced melon and rosewater drink known as *paloodeh*, as well as melon sherbets and cooling melon salads, all frequently scented with rose or orange flower water.

Sixty years after Marco Polo began his journey, the Moroccan Islamic scholar Ibn Battuta (1304–1377) travelled to Central Asia along the Silk Road. Though much less well known in the West than Polo, Ibn Battuta was one of the great world travellers. On one of his journeys Ibn Battuta visited Khwarezm in what is now Uzbekistan, where the emir lavished on him gifts of money, sable coats and beautiful horses. Ibn Battuta especially admired the melons – in this case, watermelons, although Khwarezm is famous for many different types – that he found there:

> there are no melons like Khorezmian melons, maybe with the exception of Bukharian ones, and the third best are Isfahan melons. Their peels are green, and the flesh is red, very sweet and hard. Surprisingly, they cut melons into slices, dry them in the sun, put them into baskets as it is done with Malaga figs, and take them from Khorezm to the remote cities in India and China to sell. They are the best of all dried fruit.

Another conqueror of much of the lands along the Silk Road was Timur-the-Lame (Tamerlane, 1336–1405), who may have been related to Genghis. He was a bloodthirsty soldier who left behind a trail of devastation, ruins and skulls yet was known for sumptuous meals and lavish hospitality. Ruy González de Clavijo, the Spanish ambassador to Timur, wrote of one dinner:

> Silver trenchers were filled with knots of the horse-tripe in balls the size of a fist, with a sheep's head all of a piece, served with thin cakes of their bread . . . After the roast meats came mutton stew and side dishes and the meals ended with melons and peaches and grapes, goblets of gold and silver that contained mare's milk sweetened with sugar.

The Spanish ambassador was very taken with the Central Asian melons he ate while visiting Timur – one modern scholar called him 'obsessed' – praising them as 'grande, bueno y muchos' and reporting, 'At Christmas there are so many melons and grapes it is a marvel. Each day camels laden with melons arrive, and it is a wonder how many are eaten.'

At Timur's death centralized control of the land around the Silk Road was lost. The final break of the ancient Silk Road came with the fall of Constantinople to the Ottoman Turks in 1453. Yet here, too, melons figure in the history.

The Ottoman conqueror was Sultan Mahomet II, known for his hobby of growing sweet melons at Topkapi Palace. So fond was the sultan of his melons that he was supposed to have slashed open the abdomens of fourteen servants while looking for the culprit who had stolen and eaten one of his precious melons, a story that the historian Edward Gibbon refused to believe or repeat in his *Decline and Fall of the Roman Empire*. Ottoman palace cuisine featured a delicious stuffed melon, or *dolma*. The melon was filled with buttered rice, currants, pine nuts, spices and sugar and baked to a succulent turn. Versions of this exotic *dolma* also appear in Armenian and Yemeni cooking.

The Central Asian conqueror Ẓahīr ud-Dīn Muhammad, more commonly known as Babur, was also a passionate lover of melons. Born in the fertile melon-growing region of Ferghana, near Samarkand, in 1483, Babur was a descendant of both Timur and Genghis Khan and, like them, tried to conquer Central Asia. Unlike them, he failed, but he did go on to conquer much of India, establishing what would become known as the Moghul (Mongol) Dynasty. In India in 1526–30 Babur enjoyed his newfound power but longed for Ferghana, sometimes weeping as he cut into a melon at the memories it brought. Although scientists tell us that India was the ancestral home of the melon, Babur apparently didn't think Indian melons compared much at all to those of his Central Asian home. 'There are neither good horses in India, nor good meat, nor grapes, nor melons', said the homesick conqueror in his memoirs.

Few Western travellers attempted the Silk Road in the 1500s: the dangers were too great and European explorers were distracted by the newly discovered riches of the New World. But in 1558 the English explorer and trade representative Anthony Jenkinson journeyed to Russia and then south across the Caspian Sea and into Central Asia. In Khwarezm he met a minor khan and described the land around the castle: 'The south part of this castle is low land, but very fruitful, where grow many good fruits, among which there is one called a Dynie, of a great bigness and full of moisture, which the people do eat after meat instead of drink. Also there grows another fruit called a Carbuse of the bigness of a great cucumber, yellow and sweet as sugar.' (Jenkinson seems to have had his terms mixed up – a *dynie* is a sweet melon and a *carbuse* is a watermelon in Russian dialect.) Jenkinson also noted that the river that fed the castle was drying up and the desert sand which surrounded them was encroaching on the settlement.

For the desert was reclaiming much of the Silk Road. As rivers shifted and the land grew more arid, many of the towns and oases along the Silk Road were abandoned. Some sank into dusty obscurity, and some disappeared entirely under the drifting sands. Western travel virtually ceased along the route until the great age of Victorian exploration in the nineteenth century.

One of those Victorians was the English explorer Fred Burnaby, who arrived in the Central Asian city of Khiva in the bitter cold of a winter night in the 1870s and begged hospitality at a prosperous-looking house. There he was served a sumptuous meal which, much to his surprise, included a perfect, and perfectly delicious, melon.

Melons for sale in Uzbekistan.

The climate is so dry that all the Khivans have to do to preserve their melons is to hang them up in a temperature about two degrees above freezing point . . . The melons here have a fame which is celebrated all over the East . . . Some of them attain forty pounds in weight, whilst the taste is so delicious that anyone only accustomed to this fruit in Europe would scarcely recognize its relationship with the delicate and highly perfumed melons of Khiva.

In 1882 the British journalist Edmund O'Donovan made an adventurous journey to Merv, where he was promptly detained by the Turcomen, who thought him a spy. In his journals he described how the Turcomen's teeth were serrated from the constant chewing of melon seeds and said the two best fruits of the region were

the melon and water-melon (kaoun and kharpous). The kaoun, when ripe, is of a bright golden-yellow colour, and usually fourteen or fifteen inches in length. It is very sweet, and in the hottest season preserves its interior quite cool. Before eating it the Turcomans have a curious habit of plunging it for an instant into boiling water. After this they believe that the interior is still cooler than it would otherwise be. Immense quantities are grown at Merv. The surplus not consumed during the year are stripped of the thicker portion of their rinds, cut into slices and dried in the sun. This preparation is termed kak. In taste it is very similar to a freshly dried fig, but with infinitely more aroma. The dried slices are twisted together into ropes, several feet in length, which are doubled upon themselves like rude rolls of tobacco. This is one of the few exports from Merv to Persia.

Dried, plaited melon – *kak* – still made as it has been for hundreds of years in Central Asia, but now available for online ordering.

It is interesting that travellers from Marco Polo in the 1200s to Ibn Batutta in the 1300s to O'Donovan in the late 1800s all remarked upon not only the delicious fresh melons of Central Asia, but the method of making a sweetmeat of dried melons, which was then exported for sale.

Today, although the camel caravans and caravanserai have been replaced with jets and Hilton hotels, visitors are again being welcomed on the old Silk Road. And, as they have for over 1,000 years, melons play an important role. One Chinese travel agency markets the 'Syrupy Silk Road Tour', featuring a stop at the Hami Melon Festival where over 80 varieties of melons may be tasted. In Turkmenistan August is 'Melon Month', when the favourite but most perishable melon, the *vaharman*, ripens. Melon aficionados from Russia and neighbouring countries brave the brutal August heat to come to Turkmenistan to taste this succulent *inodorus* variety of melon.

Uzbekistan is the largest zone of melon cultivation in Central Asia, with over 160 varieties being grown and 36 new varieties introduced in the last few years. Farmers in Afghanistan are hoping that one day soon their exquisitely sweet *kharbouza* melon – which is considered essential for a fine dinner party in Mumbai – will find a global as well as regional audience. Growers in Kazakhstan recently teamed up with a co-op in Germany to promote Central Asian 'sugar melons'. The romance of the Silk Road – much of it remote, uncharted or buried beneath the sands – continues to beckon, and the delicious and unusual melons of the Silk Road continue to be some of the best in the world.

6

The Melon in the Renaissance and into the Modern Era

O precious food! Delight of the mouth! Oh, much better
than gold, masterpiece of Apollo! O flower of all the fruits!
O ravishing melon!
French poet Marc-Antoine Girard, sieur de Saint-Amant (1594–1661)

Medieval Englishmen may have complained of insipid melons, but the Renaissance brought more than a flowering of
art, music and literature: it brought – apparently finally and
inarguably – truly sweet melons to the gardens and tables of
Europe, and then on to the New World. It also brought a
passion for eating them.

Melons were on the third course of the very long menu
provided to the royalty and nobility at the investiture of John
Stafford as archbishop of Canterbury in 1443. The Renais -
sance writer Bartolomeo Platina, author of the first printed
cookbook, *De honesta voluptate et valetudine* of around 1465,
reported 'with awe' that the emperor Albinus had eaten ten
Ostian melons in one sitting. Platina warned of the dangers
of eating too many melons – and was apparently proved
correct when his enemy Pope Paul II gorged on melons one
sultry night in 1471 and promptly died of apoplexy. (It was
rumoured that Paul actually died while being sodomized by

a young page, but the melon explanation was more generally acceptable, if less titillating.) Pope Paul was supposed to have been very fond of a melon soup as prepared by early Renaissance celebrity chef Martino da Como, the recipe for which appeared in around 1460. Melons also appeared on the shopping lists that Leonardo da Vinci (1452–1519) kept in his famous notebooks.

In 1495 the French king Charles VIII began his short-lived conquest of Naples. It is reported that he brought seeds of an Armenian melon back to France from Italy, where melons were raised in the country gardens of the popes in Cantalupo 'near Rome', hence the name 'cantaloupe'. Although there are numerous villages and towns named 'Cantalupo' through-out Italy and into southern France, Cantalupo in Sabina – about 85 kilometres northeast of Rome – claims to be the source of modern European cantaloupes. Still, there are some who contest that claim, and still others who think cantaloupe melons had been introduced into Provence from Italy in the

Still-life with Fruits, possibly French, *c.* 1615.

Basket of melons (*meloni*) on one of the capitals at the Palazzo Ducale in Venice.

late fourteenth or early fifteenth century, when the papacy was located in Avignon.

What we do know is that cantaloupes and other sweet melons were extremely popular in Europe from the 1500s onwards. The Cavaillon region of southern France became famous for its cantaloupe melons, supposedly descended from the melons imported from Armenia, which are still grown and celebrated to this day. Melons were the subjects of voluptuous paintings, such as the frescoes illustrating the heavenly adventures of Cupid and Psyche that decorated the Roman Villa Farnesina, completed in the early sixteenth century. The festoons surrounding the paintings are full of lush, fecund cucurbit images, including watermelons, canta-loupes (four different types) and two types of muskmelon. Caravaggio and Campi frequently used melons – round, ripe and bursting with juice – as the subjects of still-life paintings.

Thomas Coryat of England described his trip to Venice in the late 1500s and his encounter there with sweet melons:

Likewise they had another speciall commodity when I was there, which is one of the most delectable dishes for a Sommer fruite of all Christendome, namely muske Melons. I wondred at the plenty of them; for there was such store brought into the citie every morning and evening for the space of a moneth together, that not onely St Markes place, but also all the market places of the citie were superabundantly furnished with them: insomuch that I thinke there were sold so many of them every day for that space, as yeelded five hundred pound sterling. They are of three sorts, yellow, greene, and redde, but the red is most toothsome of all.

In 1609 it was reported that the agricultural areas of Sicily were renowned for their sweet melons, in particular a yellow melon that could be picked and enjoyed in the summer but could also be hung in nets and stored for winter usage.

Coryat described watermelons in Italy as 'the coldest fruit in taste that ever I did eate: the pith of it, which is in the middle, is as redde as blood, and full of blacke kernels. The Venetians find a notable commodity of it in the summer, for the cooling of themselves in time of heate. For it hath the most refrigerating virtue of all the fruites of Italy.' Two hundred years later Alexandre Dumas would agree, saying, 'The Neopolitan of the lower class is not wretched; for his necessities are in exact harmony with his desires. Does he wish to eat? A pizza or a slice of water-melon suffices.'

Popular recipes using melon also appeared in the Renais-sance. The chef Bartolomeo Scappi (1500–1577) had a recipe for melon torte in his famous *Opera* published in 1570. The recipe – melon pulp in a sauce thickened with egg and grated cheese, spiced with ginger and saffron and served in a pastry 'coffin' – was repeated in the Spanish translation published in

1599 and again in Lancelot de Casteau's 1604 version: *Pour faire tourte de melon a la Romaine.*

The Englishman John Gerard's famous *Herball* of 1597 lists and illustrates both watermelon and a number of different kinds of sweet melons, including what he calls muske melons, sugar melons, pear fashion melons and Spanish

The Watermelon Seller, Italian, *c.* 1830.

melons. Gerard tells us that the Queen of England's gardener had been successful in growing sweet melons for the royal table but noted sadly that he was unable to get watermelon seeds to germinate in England. He says that the watermelon – which he calls the 'Citrull Cucumber' – grows best in 'Sicilia, Apulia, Calabria and Syria'. And he adds, somewhat oddly, that the pulp of the watermelon 'next unto the barke is eaten rawe, but more commonly boiled; it yeeldeth to the body little nourishment and the same colde'. According to John Mariani, the first English dictionary mention of the word 'watermelon' appeared in 1615.

Watermelon was common enough in Russia that recipes for pickled watermelon rind were published in a book of dom-estic rules known as the *Domostroi* during the reign of Ivan the Terrible (1530–1584). Three hundred years later similar recipes were still being used: in the late nineteenth century, during the winter the Mennonites of South Russia reportedly ate watermelon pickle as their primary vegetable four nights out of seven. Watermelon and sweet melon were on the table for a feast prepared in honour of the birth of Peter I in 1672. In the mid-nineteenth century the German traveller Victor Hehn said, 'For at least two months in the year the Russian inhabitant of the steppes lives entirely upon arbuzes – such is the Tartar-Slavic name of the fruit – and a little bread.' Russians were also known to use watermelon juice as a sweetener and to ferment the juice for beer.

And in Egypt, watermelon continued to be one of the most abundant and appreciated fruits for both natives and invaders. In the mid-eighteenth century the Swedish explorer Fredrik Hasselquist said that watermelon 'served the Egyptians for meat, drink and physic. It is eaten in abundance, during the season even by the richer sort of people; but the common people . . . scarcely eat anything but these and account this

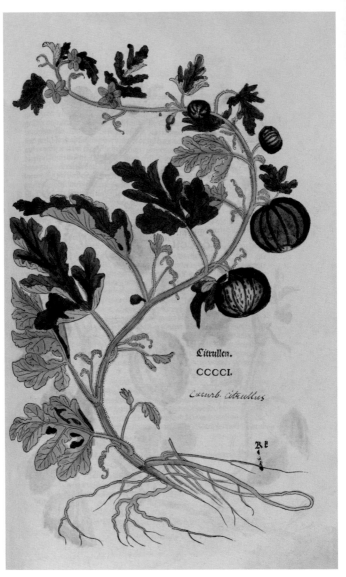

'*Citrullus lanatus* (Citrullen)', from Leonhart Fuchs's herbal *New Kreuterbuch* (1543).

Niko Pirosmani (1862–1918), *A Tatar Fruiterer.*

the best time of the year.'A few years later Napoleon's army in Egypt would have cause to be grateful for the humble water melon. According to Louis Reybaud:

> Bread and meat ran out. To supplement them, they had rice, lentils, and especially a water-melon common on the banks of the Nile, and known in our southern provinces under the name *pastèque*. This fruit, more refreshing than substantial, consoled our troops on their painful march; it became for the soldiers the object of a singular cult; in their gratitude they named it holy watermelon.

7
Melons in the New World

They have also great store of Muske-milions, Pompions,
Gourds, Cucumbers, Peason and Beanes of every colour,
yet differing from ours.

French explorer Jacques Cartier describing gardens in Canada in 1535

On his second trip to the New World islands of the Caribbean,
Christopher Columbus noted in his logbook of 29 March
1494 that he had planted melon seeds. Shortly thereafter he
marvelled that he found melons 'already grown, fit to eat, tho'
it was not above two months since the seed was put into the
ground'. The sweet melons that Columbus introduced to
the New World – and that the Spaniards would introduce into
California – were probably watermelons and muskmelons
rather than the true cantaloupe, judging by the popular melon
varieties still grown in the western hemisphere. New World
indigenous peoples may not have been overly fond of their
Old World visitors and conquerors, but they took to Old
World melons with great alacrity and the fruit spread very
rapidly.

Melons 'different from those here' were described in
Central America as early as 1516 by Pascual de Andagoya.
The Spaniard Francisco López de Gómara described melons

The very successful Montreal melon, possibly descended from one of the muskmelon varieties Cartier observed in 1535, in an 1887 advertisement.

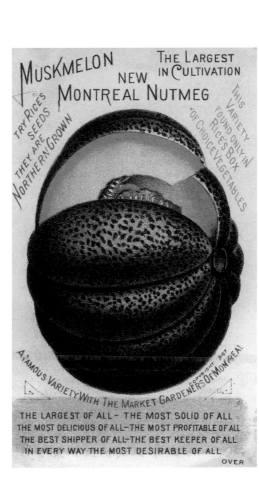

in New Mexico in 1540 where the Spanish named the rose red mountains there 'Sandia', or 'watermelon mountains'. The Spaniards also reported watermelons in Florida in 1576. By 1609 melons were purportedly growing along the Hudson River in New York. In Salem, Massachusetts, the Reverend Francis Higginson in 1628 wrote of cultivating 'musk-millions, water-millions . . . and many other odde fruits that I cannot name'. According to Father Marquette, melons were being cultivated in Illinois by 1673 and he pronounced their taste

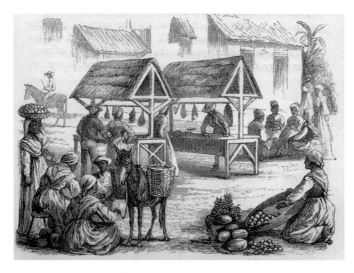

Watermelons and other fruit being sold at the market in Santo Domingo in the Caribbean, 1873.

'excellent'. In 1683 the Spanish brought melon seeds to California.

Melon culture in the Spanish colonies of North America was very successful. The hot sun, combined with irrigation techniques taught by the Spanish, made for plentiful and delicious sweet melons and watermelons. In 1601 a Spanish witness reported that the Pueblo Indians in New Mexico were raising maize, beans, calabashes and melon with the help of irrigation canals. The Pueblos not only grew melons for eating fresh but preserved thick-skinned varieties in cool earth cellars to eat during the winter. On Christmas Day 1864 Mamie Bernard from Kansas was served a root-cellared watermelon in New Mexico and was amazed to find it 'as fresh and crisp as if it had just been cut'.

Pueblo Indians also were known to twist muskmelon flesh into ropes and dry it in the sun – the same technique used by Central Asians and noted by Marco Polo hundreds of years earlier. By the early 1900s the Pueblos were selling melons to outsiders. Crop reports from 1890 show that 15,000 Pueblo melons had been raised, while by 1900 the number was over 145,000. In 1910 when the train passed through New Mexico, girls with wagons full of muskmelons and watermelons sold their produce to the passengers for five cents each, but demanded ten cents for the watermelons.

Melons and watermelons were common in early colonial Panama and Peru as well as in British and Dutch colonies throughout the New World. African crops such as plantains, tamarind and watermelon were tended by slaves on a sugar plantation in Barbados in 1648 and watermelon was cultivated in slave gardens in Brazil by 1648. And it was watermelon seed from Brazil that was taken to Tahiti on Captain Cook's first voyage in 1769. Watermelon may also have been planted in Australia on Cook's first voyage there.

Wasser-limonene (watermelons), illustrated after plants seen growing in Brazil by German soldier and explorer Caspar Schmalkalden in the mid-1600s.

African slaves are credited in many accounts with introducing watermelon to the New World, the slaves supposedly smuggling the seeds in their hair. Since the first slaves arrived in 1619 and watermelon was growing all over the New World by then, African slavery doesn't seem to have been the primary agency. Nevertheless African slave centres throughout the New

Drawing of a Surinamese watermelon, *c.* 1705, by Maria Sibylla Merian, who described the flesh as shiny and said that it 'melts in the mouth like sugar; it is healthy and has a very pleasant taste'.

World usually had watermelon as a crop. Whether particular varieties had travelled from Africa with the slaves or whether watermelon simply flourished in the same hot climates as slavery – or both – we don't yet know.

John Stedman described melons growing in the slave-owning Dutch colony of Surinam in northeastern South America in the late eighteenth century:

> The musk and water-melons grow also plentifully in this country; the first is of a globular form, large, like the crown of a small hat, ribbed, buff colour, orange and green. The pulp is yellow, firm, sweet and succulent; still it is eaten with sugar, but more frequently with black pepper and salt – the smell of the fruit is excellent. The water-melon is of an oval or cylindrical shape, its colour is a bright polished green, and partly a very pale buff; the pulp of the fruit is a pink colour and of a mellow watery substance; its taste is sweet, exceedingly cooling, and of a most agreeable flavour.

Watermelon and sweet melons were especially popular in the slave-holding areas of what would become the United States. In the Virginia colony there in 1737 John Custis, a rela-tive of George Washington's wife, said that 'his Negroes' specialized in making 'multitudes of melons'. During the U.S. Civil War (1861–5) farmers in the blockaded slave-holding South made molasses and sugar from melons.

8
The Deadly Melon

> But I advise thee . . . to abstaine from the immoderate eating
> of them. For the sweetnesse of them is such as hath allured
> many men to eate so immoderately of them, that they have
> therewith hastened their untimely death, the fruite being indeed
> . . . sweete-sowre. Sweete in the palate, but sowre in the
> stomacke, if it be not soberly eaten. For it doth often breede
> the Dysenteria, that is, the bloudy fluxe; of which disease
> the Emperour Fredericke the Third died by the intemperate
> eating of them.
>
> Thomas Coryat, an Englishman travelling in Venice in the early 1500s

Early writings on melons were full of warnings of the deadly results that awaited the innocent eater. As mentioned previously, Platina reported in 1471 that Pope Paul had died of apoplexy brought on by eating two very large melons. In 1681 the governor of Nuevo León in Mexico died suddenly. The cause of death given was overindulging in cantaloupes and watermelons. In the 1720s Peter the Great of Russia ordered his troops in Persia to stop eating melons because he thought they were the cause of the great fevers his army was suffering.

Melons were considered not only dangerous but dangerously alluring: the English historian and traveller William

Thomas observed in the 1500s that 'their sweetness is so attractive that no one can resist it and some even eat so many that they die as a result.' The sixteenth-century Italian poet Antonio Mario Negrisoli warned of the sexual dangers of melon, saying it 'excites all desires . . . and is Ganymede's favourite food'. John Gerard in his *Herball* of 1597 warned against the dangerous melon, as well, saying that it was

> harder of digestion then is any of the rest of Cucumbers: & if it remaine long in the stomack it putrifieth, and is occasion of pestilent agues, which thing also Aetius witnesseth in the first book of his Tetrables, writing that the use of Cucumeres . . . breedeth pestilent feavers; for he also taketh Cucumis to be that which is commonly called Melon: which is usually eaten of the Italians and Spaniards, rather to represse the rage of lust, then any other Phisical virtue.

But why were melons considered so dangerous? In the West, the answer goes back at least to ancient times. Medicine from Hippocrates (460–377 BC) onwards had been dominated by the theory that the human body was filled with four substances, or humours, each with its own characteristic traits: blood (sanguine); yellow bile (choleric); black bile (melancholic); and phlegm (phlegmatic). All foods could be divided into four categories – hot, cold, wet and dry – which needed to be manipulated to balance the different bodily humours to promote or restore health. Melons were considered cold and wet and needed to be balanced by hot, dry elements, such as aged cheese, vinegar, salt or cured meats. Traditional Chinese medicine had similarities to the humoral theory. It classified foods as warm, mild, cool or cold but, like the Western humoral theory, was not looking at the temperature of the food itself

The classic Italian dish of *prosciutto di Parma* with melon, which has roots in ancient and medieval medicine.

but at its effects on the body. Watermelon was considered cold by nature and therefore very dangerous to pregnant women, as the cold might kill the foetus.

In addition to the humoral theory, which classified melons as cold and wet, there was another theory developed during the early Middle Ages, known as the 'Chain of Being', which ranked all of creation, including plants, on how close each was to God. Melons, growing along the ground as they did, were at one of the lowest rungs of the chain, and therefore somewhat suspect. If melons were eaten at all, they were best consumed at the beginning of the meal so they would not putrefy in the stomach. Hence our 'modern' starter (appetizer) of melon wrapped in prosciutto, reflecting the humoral theory of balancing cold melon with the hot/dry prosciutto and the Chain of Being theory of consuming melon at the least dangerous place in a meal.

We might smile at the idea that melons could be dangerous to the stomach and even cause death, but those old-fashioned ideas were not necessarily off-base. Melons grow on the ground, often in contact with animal – or human – manures. Rough-skinned melons can pick up *E. coli* and other contaminants very easily and if they are not cleaned thoroughly before they are cut and consumed, the contaminants may easily enter the body, causing serious illness. In 2004 a number of deaths in North America were traced to *E. coli* transmitted via muskmelons. After the outbreak, so potent was the fear of sickness and death from melons that u.s. growers tried to get their government to declare the watermelon not technically a melon in order to distance watermelons – which are not quite so likely to harbour bacteria on their smoother skins – from the food safety issues.

Even though melons were considered dangerous, their powerful properties could be harnessed for the body's good. In medieval Byzantium the natures of melons were described so that the educated could use them to best advantage. As Andrew Dalby translates in *Flavours of Byzantium*,

Sweet melons predispose towards and produce 'cholera'. They have a moist and cold nature, they quench thirst and cool the heat of the liver and stomach. They are unsuited to those with cold constitutions. They have a cleansing quality: they provoke urination, moisten the bowels and produce semen. When not fully ripe they act as emetics, especially if eaten in large quantity. Water - melons are not as moist or as productive of bad humours as melons, and are not so diuretic or so effective as emetics.

Although not as good to eat as other fruits, they are better to eat than melons.

Since ancient times, dangerous but powerful melons have been considered beneficial against kidney stones and for protecting the body against heatstroke. They have also been recommended against high blood pressure, gout, macular degeneration and cataracts. Bitter melon has been used in traditional Hindu Ayurvedic medicine against diabetes. An Islamic hadith said (contra Chinese traditional medicine), 'None of your women who are pregnant and eat of watermelon will fail to produce offspring who are good in countenance and good in character', and the Santería religion of West African and Caribbean origin prescribed watermelon for improved eyesight.

Melon seeds have been used as medicine for centuries, as well. The thirteenth-century *Andalusian Cookbook* contains a recipe for a syrup of hyssop that includes watermelon seeds, which was used to help a cough, cure brain abcesses, dissolve phlegm and cause urine and menstrual blood to flow. The Moor Ibn Zuhr (Avenzoar) prescribed watermelon hearts for fevers, and melon-seed broth to prevent or treat kidney stones. Melon seeds are still thought to be healthful and in Iran and China are consumed not only as tasty snacks but to control hypertension.

Yet the old fears about the danger of melons lingered into the modern era, though it is doubtful that those who professed that fear had any idea that they were expressing ancient and medieval medical practice. In 1867 the *American Hand-book of Practical Cookery, for Ladies and Professional Cooks* warned:

> Musk-melons are always served as a hors-d'oeuvre, but must be eaten immediately after soup, or the first thing

of all if no soup is served. It is a great mistake to serve melons as a dessert. Water-melons, though eaten abundantly, are considered very unwholesome by the great majority of doctors, chemists, and physiologists.

The noted English food writer Elizabeth David said in 1970 that in her childhood 'it was customary to hand round a bowl of powdered ginger when melon was served . . . to counteract [its] chilling effects.'

Still, today, most of the world looks on melons and water - melons as delicious, nutritious, cooling foods to enjoy on a hot day. The fruits are low in carbohydrates – the bugaboo of modern Westerners – devoid of cholesterol and nearly devoid of fats, and are a good source of vitamin C. Yellow, orange and green melons are high in vitamin A, red water-melons are a good source of lycopene and all melons provide potassium, along with various types of B vitamins, such as folate and niacin. Melons contain minimal amounts of sodium

Melon seeds, a satisfying and nutritious snack.

but have plenty of trace minerals. In Moscow, when melon season rolls around and melons from all over the former Soviet Union flood the markets, Russians line up at markets and spas to partake in a yearly late summer cleansing of the body. 'The torpedo melons clean out the bowels, and the watermelons clean out the urinary and genital systems', one Muscovite explained. In recent years melon extracts have even become popular in expensive skin treatment regimens to promote a youthful glow, some of these promoted by glamorous celebrities.

Yet one of the best ways to enjoy melons seems to have been described by E. W. Lane in 1836 as he travelled through Egypt:

> A dish of watermelon (*bateekh*) if in season generally forms part of the meal. This is cut up about a quarter of an hour before and left to cool in the external air, or in a current of air, by the evaporation of the juices on the surface of the slices; but it is always watched during this time, lest a serpent should come to it and poison it by its breath or bite, for this reptile is said to be extremely fond of the water-melon, and to smell it at a great distance. Water-melons are very abundant in Egypt and mostly very delicious and wholesome.

9
Folk Tales and
Humorous Stories

Oh, plant a watermelon vine upon my grave
And let the juice (slurp slurp) seep through
Oh, plant a watermelon vine upon my grave
That's all I ask of you
American children's camp song

Melons, especially watermelons, are liberally represented in folk tales and funny stories from around the globe. In their study of cucurbits in literature, Ralf Norrman and Jon Haarberg argue that 'in regions where cucurbits grow easily and manual work is despised, cucurbits develop negative class connotations.' Large curcubits – such as melons, watermelons and pumpkins – also appeal to our sense of humour, perhaps because of the likeness to an oversized human head that melons and pumpkins share, and the undignified way in which many watermelons are eaten. Whatever the cause, melons and watermelons are often the nexus around which humorous stories of foolish humanity are written.

An Armenian story tells of a lowly villager who cracks open a stolen watermelon and eats the red, juicy heart. 'Let passersby think that a king was here and ate the best of the melon', he says. Still hungry, the man eats the rest of the melon

A melon falls from on high in a fruit market, hitting a female customer on the head, in a humorous lithograph published in the early 1800s.

pulp, saying, 'Let passersby think the king's servant ate the second best part of the melon.' Finally he eats every last piece of the watermelon rind. 'Let passersby think the king's horse finished off that melon.'

Another story, from Turkey this time, tells of the legendary Hoca, a comic figure from the medieval era. While the Hoca is sitting in his garden under the shade of a walnut tree, he notices how spindly the watermelon vine is compared to the size of the watermelon fruit. 'Why didn't God make big watermelons grow in big trees and little walnuts on little vines?' wonders the Hoca. Just then, a walnut falls from the tree and hits the Hoca on the head. 'How wise God is for arranging the world as he has done!' exclaims the Hoca.

Also linking watermelons and fools is a story from Guyana about two friends who buy a load of watermelons for $5 each, then turn around and sell them at the market for $5 each. When one friend complains about the lack of profit, the other friend exclaims, 'See, I told you we should have bought more watermelons!'

In the United States, the humorous and undignified aspect of watermelon eating was used, especially in the American South after the Civil War, as a symbol to dehumanize African Americans. A typical example comes from a biography of a Southern planter written in 1887, where the suitably grateful blacks praise their generous white betters – in dialect, of course:

> Mrs Henderson was so good to her people. An' we used to go down dyar to de Pint, all dressed up an' set back on dem pleasurin' benches. Mrs Henderson had a big watermillion patch ebery year, an' she let her people hab all dey want. An' dey cut a heap ov 'em for we all, an' we sot back on dem benches an' we eat jes' as long as we could. Oh, I'se been see good times!

A whole American industry grew up around 'humorous' racist cartoons, postcards, salt and pepper shakers, and small souvenirs that depicted African Americans as simpletons who just couldn't help loving watermelon. So strong was this connection that, to this day, some African Americans will not eat watermelon in public. (This may explain the statistic published by the U.S. Department of Agriculture showing that African Americans buy fewer watermelons than any other racial group in the United States.) So prevalent is the association still that a 'humorous' email of an image showing the White House lawn covered with watermelons went viral when Barack Obama was elected U.S. president in 2009.

Melons were often linked to stories of morality and the contrast between good and evil, rich and poor. There is a Korean folk story about two brothers, one rich and one poor, who learn the value of family love via a small bird and a melon seed. A very similar Russian story also features two brothers – one a selfish rich man, the other a kind-hearted poor man – and a bird that brings a magical melon seed. When the magical seed is planted, the melons that grow bring riches to the poor brother and destruction to the rich one.

A Hmong folk tale tells the story of a poor childless farmer and his wife who work and work all year in their garden but are dismayed to find that the only result is one large winter melon. The two old people are distraught – until the melon speaks and announces that he is their new son, Winter Melon Boy. Winter Melon Boy grows into a handsome young man who helps the old man and his wife around the garden, greatly increasing their comfort. But the good times come to an end when war breaks out and the local mandarin demands that Winter Melon Boy join the army to fight. When the elderly couple protest that their son is only a melon, the mandarin demands money instead. The farmer and his wife are downcast, until Winter Melon Boy turns dog excrement into golden nuggets, thrilling the mandarin, who orders all the gold brought to his storehouse, where he gloats over the nuggets. Winter Melon Boy is saved from fighting in the war and goes off with his happy parents. When the mandarin's golden nuggets eventually turn back into dog excrement, Winter Melon Boy and his parents are nowhere to be found.

Strange stories have often been attached to melons. Travel - lers in Astrakhan in the south of Russia told of a melon that grew in the shape of a lamb, eating the grass beneath itself and rolling over to find more pasture. It had a furry pelt that could be cured to make clothing. Even more amazing, this

Poster advertising a minstrel show, U.S., *c.* 1900.

melon was able to trap wolves – the only animal that would eat its flesh.

A Ming Daoist story tells of an immortal disguised as an old gardener who digs a melon out of the snow, startling his human companions:

'Carving One of Our Watermelons', photograph by William H. Martin, 1909, postcard spoofing the blandishments land companies used to lure settlers to the middle of the United States.

With green leaves, a tender stalk, and yellow flowers blooming at the top. From its pungent source rose its fragrance; from bitterness came its sweet taste . . . The old man took a knife and peeled the melon and cut off the top, letting out an extraordinary fragrance . . . 'How very strange!' they exclaimed. How could he have grown such sweet melons in such heavy snow?'

Another story, from the Uighurs in Central Asia, demonstrates how a melon brought about the marriage of a poor girl to a rich prince. The prince was given two coins by his father the king and instructed to buy seed for the chicken, food for the king's family and fodder for the donkey. The prince was confounded by this and sat by the side of the road in despair, unable to work out how to buy so many things with only two coins. Just then the beautiful daughter of a poor farmer came upon the prince and asked him what was bothering him. When he explained, the girl laughed, asked for the coins and went off, telling him she would solve his problem. When she returned with a large melon, the prince was angry. 'How can a melon help me?' demanded the prince. The girl explained that the king's family could eat the melon flesh, the chickens could eat the seeds and the donkey could eat the rind. The prince ran back happily to his father with the melon, explaining how he had provided so much food for only two coins, but the king doubted that his son could have been so clever. After questioning the young man, the king sent for the poor girl and married the prince to her.

A Vietnamese story is interesting not only for its charm, but because it claims that watermelon was introduced to Vietnam in the first millennium BC. According to the legend a Hong prince named Mai An Tiêm was exiled to a small island but was told that if he could survive for six months, his exile would end. As the prince prayed for help, a bird flew past and dropped a seed. The prince planted the seed and soon a delicious watermelon grew that sustained the prince until his exile was over. When An Tiêm returned home, he taught his people to grow watermelons, which he called 'western melon', since the bird came from the west. The Vietnamese celebrate every New Year with watermelon, remembering Prince An Tiêm's gift.

Sometimes the stories are just for fun, as in the story of the saucy farmer who made a king laugh. The story goes that a king was travelling incognito in the north of India to see how his subjects lived. When he reached the farm of a poor Jatt man, the king was hungry and thirsty and asked the Jatt for a melon. 'No, they are not for sale', the Jatt replied. 'I am going to present my melons to the king.' The king was taken aback and asked, 'What if the king does not accept your present?' The Jatt replied, 'Then the king can go to hell.' A few days later, the Jatt journeyed to the king's court to present his melons. When he saw the king, he recognized him at once as his thirsty visitor. 'Well, Jatt, I see you have brought these melons for me', the king said. 'But what if I do not accept them?' The Jatt thought for a minute, then replied, 'Your majesty already knows the answer.' The king laughed heartily at the Jatt's wit and gave him a large reward for his melons.

And sometimes the fun comes in the shape of a riddle, as in this one from Persia:

What is that which is round and rolling?
Its whole without life but its halves alive?
An ass is he who cannot answer this
And less than a goat is that ass.
Answer: A melon

10

Festivals, Contests and Folk Art

To be in a watermelon patch on a hot summer night in the tropics
is a strange experience. The air is filled with whispers and noises:
the melons grow not only visibly but audibly, creating noise as
the vines creep over the ground.

Ralf Norrman and Jon Haarberg, 1980

In the thirteenth century the Islamic scholar and traveller Al-
Qazvini wrote that the watermelons of Aswan in Egypt were
so large that a strong camel could carry only two. Modern-day
watermelons can be even bigger.

In 2011 Chris Kent of Sevierville, Tennessee, in the southern United States, said of his Guinness World Record-winning
291-lb (132-kg) watermelon that it was gaining 5 or 6 lb a day
(2.3–2.7 kg) at its peak. 'You know, it's just the "wow" factor.
You go out one day and then you go out the next, and you
can really see that it has grown. It is really amazing.' That
bigness, that 'wow factor', gets people excited and gets them
entering contests. And then one thing leads to another and
fun ensues.

Hope, Arkansas, bills itself as the 'Home of President Bill
Clinton, Governor Mike Huckabee and the World's Largest
Watermelons' and has been hosting its Watermelon Festival

since the mid-1920s. In addition to lots of ice-cold watermelon slices, the festival features the 'Watermelon Olympics', which includes the team watermelon toss, the ever popular seed-spitting contest and a watermelon-eating competition, not to mention the 'Watermelon Idol' event. Hope's claim to the largest watermelons rests with the Bright family, who have had Guinness-certified whoppers three times (in 1979, 1985 and 2005).

Lloyd Bright, who also runs the family's seed company, Giant Watermelons, in Hope, started growing big melons in 1973 with the Carolina Cross cultivar, the most popular and reliable of the 'giant' varieties. He says he can usually spot a championship-size melon right away because the fruit starts out bigger and keeps outpacing its neighbours, but lots of sun and a good water supply play crucial roles, too. At the moment, he says, most of the watermelon-growing contests take place in the U.S., but as the fun of growing giant watermelons spreads to countries like Australia and South Africa, the contests follow. Interestingly, he also says that while in the past the biggest giant watermelons have been grown in the southern U.S., global warming is bringing in competition from more northern states. As for the rumour that giant water - melons are big in size but short on taste, Bright swears it isn't so. 'If they're grown right and picked ripe, they are sweet and delicious', he says. Bright will continue to get competition from Chris Kent, who is not content with the award-winning watermelons he's grown so far. His goal: a 700-lb (318-kg) watermelon.

Also claiming the title of home of the world's largest watermelons is Daxing, China. The Watermelon Museum in Daxing hosts an annual festival where farmers from all over the province bring their watermelons to be judged. In 2003 a watermelon weighing 264 lb (120 kg) was said to have been auctioned for 1 million yuan (U.S.$120,482). And, says the *China Daily*, 'a watermelon eating contest is another unusual attraction during the festival. The person who gobbles the most, fast, wins.' The attempt to grow large watermelons caused big problems in China's Jiangsu province in 2011. Farmers were treating the young fruit with a growth chemical that caused the mature fruit to explode. Needless to say, markets were hesitant about buying watermelons that would burst open unexpectedly and most of that year's crop had to be thrown out.

Although they don't grow as spectacularly big as watermelons, sweet melons are also grown for size. As unlikely as it sounds, snowy Palmer, Alaska, was the spot where a world-record-winning 64.8-lb (29.4-kg) muskmelon was grown in 2004.

Queensland is the biggest watermelon-growing area in Australia and celebrates the fruit with its biennial Chinchilla Melon Festival in February. Events there include melon skiing, melon iron man, melon bungee, melon bullseye, seed-spitting

Statue to the watermelon, Weatherford, Texas, 1939.

Gorging on melons at the Diyarbakir melon festival, 1990s.

and melon tossing. One of its more unusual events also landed a Guinness World Record in 2009 when the contestant John Allwood smashed 47 watermelons in 60 seconds using nothing but his own head. Argentina holds a national watermelon festival every year and in Brazil, in the state of Rio Grande Do Sul, watermelon is the symbol of Our Lady of the Navigators and is a feature of its yearly festival.

Watermelons are in high demand every autumn in Saskatchewan, Canada, when the Roughriders football team plays. Fans hollow out the melons, wearing them as helmets and sometimes even as bikinis. '[They have] taken all the watermelons available in Western Canada', said David Karwacki, CEO of the Saskatoon-based fruit and vegetable wholesaler Star Produce. 'You just can't get them there quick enough.'

Sweet melon festivals also take place around the globe. Howell, Michigan, has been celebrating its unique American cantaloupe variety since 1960 with a Melon Ball dance, canta - loupe ice cream and a long-distance run held as a fundraiser for local charities. Cavaillon, France, goes melon mad when its famous melons come into season in July. The second of August is Melon Day in Turkmenistan and is not only a festival day but a national public holiday. In Tajikistan over 150 tons of melons were featured at the Honey and Melon festival in

Master watermelon carver Takashi Itoh's carving of artist Vincent van Gogh.

Day of the Dead (Día de los Muertos) model of the Last Supper, with the skeletal disciples eating watermelon.

2012, and in Qatar, the first Lulu Melon Festival was launched in April 2014.

Melons and watermelons are also popular in art, both fine and folk. From Caravaggio's canvases in the early 1600s featuring lush melons, to ceramics and paintings from Mexico showing watermelon being eaten by the dead as part of the Día de los Muertos celebration, melons' rounded and volup-tuous shapes and bold colours appeal to artists of all stripes. One of the more interesting folk art forms dealing with melons is made with the actual melon itself.

How exactly it got started is anyone's guess, but melon carving, particularly watermelon carving, has become high art. The annual Melounovy European Melon Carving Festival, which began in 2006 in the Czech Republic, is 'ground zero' for melon carving and draws the best watermelon artists from around the world. Master carver Takashi Itoh of Japan credits the ancient fruit and vegetable sculpture tradition of Thailand as the primary influence on his technique. Thai carving sets, along with other specialized carving knives and tools, are available from a number of speciality companies, and cooking schools are teaching chefs the art of vegetable and fruit carving in general – including carved carrots, turnips and sweet melons – but of course the watermelon offers a beguilingly large canvas. The Food Network cable television channel now features a Fantasy Food Sculpture challenge. The winning sculpture in 2008 stood over 6 feet (2 m) tall and featured four intricately carved watermelons. Carved melons – again, especially watermelons – are suggested centrepieces for large parties and receptions. In addition to their beauty and conversation-piece value, carved melons hold up much better over long periods in warm rooms than the traditional ice sculptures of old.

II

Modern and Future Melons

The hot, humid Indian subcontinent may be the ancestral home of the sweet melon and hot, dry Africa may be the home of the watermelon, but melons are the most successful warm weather fruit crop worldwide – and can be grown, with a bit of help, nearly everywhere. Truly, melons have come a long way on their journey with humankind.

Production in China far outdistances any other region, accounting for over half of world production by weight. The other top melon-producing countries are Spain, Iran, Turkey, the USA, Romania, Italy, Morocco, India and Egypt. In 2006, China was producing over 60,000,000 metric tons of watermelon per year – some of which were raised for seeds for snacking – as well as large quantities of sweet melons, especially the Hami type, along with wax gourds (winter melon) and bitter melons. Turkey produces nearly 4 million tons of watermelon, as well as snake melon and many kinds of sweet melon, especially canta - loupe and *inodorus* types; total production is over 1,765,600 tons. So popular did watermelon become in Brazil that the country is considered a major centre of diversity and is fourth in the world in total watermelon production. The U.S. is the greatest importer of sweet melons worldwide and Germany is the larg- est importer of watermelons, followed by the U.S. and Canada.

Melon production is still impacted by the migration of peoples, just as it was in prehistory. In the late nineteenth century Armenian immigrants to the hot, fertile valleys of central California flourished in their adopted country, growing sweet casaba and Persian melons from their Asian homeland. Nearly 100 years later, émigrés from Afghanistan and Central Asia are trying their hand at raising exotic sweet melons from their home countries in California. So far, results are mixed, due to disease-resistance problems and the difficulty of getting highly perishable melons to market quickly enough, but the melons are unique and delicious enough that the farmers as well as their speciality shop clients appear to want to keep trying. Bitter melon seems to have travelled to the New World with the African slave trade and is now a popular vegetable in the Caribbean and Latin America. Immigrants from the Indian subcontinent and Asia have brought bitter melons to the markets of Toronto and Vancouver in Canada. Improving the quality of melons is also an ongoing goal for many producers.

The sweet and fragrant galia melon – a cross between a honeydew and a muskmelon – was developed in Israel in the 1970s and is now grown commercially in Brazil, Spain, the u.s., Panama, Egypt and Costa Rica. In France locally grown, exquisitely delicious sweet melons are a matter of national pride. In Cavaillon the local cantaloupe is so esteemed that in 1864 Alexandre Dumas donated all 194 of his published works to the library at Cavaillon on the condition that he be given twelve of the famous melons every year until the end of his life. In 1987 La Confrérie des chevaliers de l'ordre du melon (The Brotherhood of Knights of the Order of the Melon) was inaugurated, with the mission of celebrating, preserving, improving and promoting the Charentais melons of Cavaillon. Restaurant Prévôt in Cavaillon – which was

La Confrérie des chevaliers de l'ordre du melon parade in Vaucluse, France.

awarded a Michelin star in 2013 – features the local melon in season, from June to September, with dishes such as *Entremêlé de sole et de melon aux épices douces* (sole with melon and sweet spices), *Rosace de melon et tartare de chèvre frais* (melon with young goat cheese) and *Melon cocotte au homard* (melon and lobster).

Spain produces many types of watermelon and sweet melon, but its best-known melon is the piel de sapo (toad skin). This melon – an *inodorus* type – has crisp, white, sweet flesh with a wrinkled green rind, hence the descriptive name. The piel de sapo was developed in Spain but the Spanish market for it is so large that many are now grown in Brazil and Central America for export back to the home country. A little-known Spanish speciality is the *inodorus* variety Amarillo Oro, or 'yellow gold'. The rind is golden but the interior is a beautiful combination of peach, white and green, and the taste

Melons for sale in Cavaillon.

Watermelon delivery in Shanghai.

of its succulent, juicy flesh is described by the melon grower and connoisseur Amy Goldman as 'sheer delight'.

In North America producers are looking at exotic imports from Central Asia, but also at some of the heritage melons that were grown in the past. The Montreal melon is a case in point. This melon, which interestingly enough may be a descendant of a melon carried to Canada from France by Jesuits in the late seventeenth century, was brought to full development in the 1800s. It was a large netted melon with green flesh and an exquisite, spicy perfume. By the 1880s Burpee Seeds, one of the largest American seed companies, distributed it as one of their most popular varieties in the u.s. Unfortunately the Montreal melon, like many melons of those days, would start to rot as soon as three days off the vine, making it unsuitable for industrial production – which was taking over farming in North America – and so its popularity dropped off. By the mid-twentieth century it appeared to be extinct. But in 1995 seeds were found in a seed bank in Iowa and efforts began to bring this delicious melon back into production. So far, results are mixed, with the new melons still much smaller than the original, but growers are working on improving the resurrected Montreal melon. In South Carolina in the southern United States, Professor David Shields has been working with farmers and growers to revive the 180-year-old Bradford watermelon, once thought extinct, but recently discovered still growing in the backyard of the Bradford family. Shields helped to organize the production of molasses from the Bradford melons, the first time this had been done since the end of the u.s. Civil War (1860–65). The flavour of the molasses was deep and sweet, yet floral, according to Shields, who says of the Bradford melon: 'of all the lost melons of yesteryear, this is the one I wished would return. And it has. It's the taste of the past but it's also the taste of the future.'

The sheer enjoyment of melons seems to be a worldwide phenomenon. The distinctive Densuke watermelon, which grows only on the Japanese island of Hokkaido, typically sells for between u.s.$180 and $300 each. Only about 9,000 of the nearly black melons are grown each year, and every year the largest melon is auctioned off to support local agriculture. In 2008 a 17-lb (7.7-kg) Densuke – with its crisp hard flesh that is supposed to taste like a watermelon but 'different' – was sold for an astounding u.s.$6,100. Japan is also the country where in 2008 twin Yubari melons were auctioned off for a record-breaking u.s.$23,500. The Yubari is a muskmelon cultivar also grown in Hokkaido and considered the 'Cadillac' of sweet melons in Japan, where it is often given as a gift in special melon presentation boxes. Japan has pioneered square watermelons and muskmelons, grown in special glass containers to shape the fruit. Square melons are easy to stack and store but are considerably more expensive than standard melons. One enterprising Japanese couple has recently developed a heart-shaped watermelon, which sold for u.s.$160 each in 2012.

A square watermelon in Japan priced at u.s.$300.

Melon seeds – sometimes a by-product, sometimes a purposeful crop – also are important around the world. M. M. Bandhari described a melon crop in 1970s India:

> The pulp of the watermelon is much consumed, being eaten fresh. The seeds are dried and pounded into a flour which is then mixed with the flour of Bajra, to prepare cakes called Sogra. These small flat seeds when dried are said to taste like almonds. In normal years the fruits are available in such plenty that many are thrown to the cattle.

In various parts of Africa the egusi melon – a not-very-tasty watermelon cousin – is grown specifically for its seeds, which provide inexpensive protein and oil and are an important dietary supplement. Asia also produces large amounts of edible melon seeds, both as a snack item and ground as an ingredient in such foods as the famous Chinese moon cakes.

It is true that many of the world's best melons can only be enjoyed close to where they are grown because the delicate fruit simply won't tolerate shipping and/or storage. Growers in Afghanistan believe they can compete successfully against the opium poppy crop and the devastation of war with their delicious torpedo-shaped *inodorus* melons, but so far they have not been able to get enough of the melon crop to market before it rots, in order to make a profit. And sometimes, the best laid plans of melon growers . . . A few years ago in Nigeria a combination of a bumper crop of watermelons and a break-down in the transportation system resulted in thousands of melons rotting by the roadside, while just a few miles away the markets were empty of watermelons.

Growers and researchers such as Donald N. Maynard and Deena Decker-Walters in the u.s. and Harry Paris in Israel, as well as scientists in Uganda, Uzbekistan, Turkey, Sudan, Nigeria, Spain, Brazil and other melon-producing countries around the world, are continually working on producing delicious melons that are easy to bring to market. Some of the research focuses on breeding for such traits as resistance to fungal in-fections and blights, as well as to certain insect pests that can devastate a crop. Sometimes it involves going back to wild landraces found in Africa and India to tap into the genetic potential these hardy forbears possess for improvements to modern melons. Since, like other crops today, melons have been monocultured in many areas of the world, growers and botan - ists are concerned that genetic diversity and potential are being lost as old cultivars disappear. Organizations such as Seed Savers Exchange and Seeds of Diversity are attempting to rescue vanishing heirloom melon varieties. Many of those melon types were grown in home and market gardens as recently as the 1940s but passed out of favour because of the pressure of industrial agriculture's need for uniform crops that could be shipped or stored without damage – flavour being a smaller consideration.

One interesting area of melon breeding that is being attempted is the development of sweet melons that also contain a bit of sourness, as most other fruits do. While sourness does occur in melons, it has not been emphasized in breeding over the last few thousand years, while sweetness has – the combination of sweet and sour in one melon is an unusual idea.

The prehistory of watermelon lies in Africa, but the future of watermelon may also lie there. While most of the 100 million tons of watermelons grown in the world today are grown outside of Africa, the continent still has much to offer in the development of the fruit.

The wild African landraces of watermelon may not be much to look at, or even to taste. They are still often bitter and frequently very small. But while contests may celebrate giant watermelons, consumers are asking for smaller and smaller fruit to fit in their refrigerators and lunch boxes. A 'downsizing' gene may indeed be hidden in one of the small wild fruits still littering the desert wastes of Africa. Scientists are also looking at African wild melons for better seedless varieties, as well as for super-seeded types that could be used for the burgeoning dried melon seed market. And as geneticists worry about the lack of genetic variety in monocropping, the wild watermelons of Africa offer a ready-made genetic bank. For the !Kung San, the /Gwi San and the //Gana peoples of the Kalahari, the age-old relationship between human and food source continues, as the wild watermelon still offers a source of forage for their animals, a vegetable crop for themselves, seeds for snacking and for making meal, and a portable water supply to help them survive the dry months.

Appendix I
Picking the Perfect Melon in the Garden and the Market

An old Turkmen proverb says: 'The sweetest melon belongs to the jackal' – meaning that the animals that live near your melon plot are liable to discover that your melons are ripe before you do. So how do you beat the jackals and tell if the melon in the garden or at the market is ripe?

Muskmelons are the easiest: they will 'slip' from the vine when ripe. At the market, you can look to see if the muskmelon has been cut off the vine, in which case it was probably picked before maturity. Other varieties of sweet melon must be judged by the shape, size, feel, colour and aroma of the fruit. Look for a melon that feels heavy for its size and has a pleasing aroma (if it should have an aroma) and the colour expected at ripeness. If you put slight pressure at the blossom end of the fruit and it gives, that is a sign of ripeness as well. If you have grown the melon yourself, you can also judge maturity by the amount of time the fruit has been on the vine against its reported date.

Watermelons have no aroma by which to judge ripeness, but there are a few clues to look for: the spot on the underside of the melon where it lies on the ground will begin to turn from white to light yellow. The tendril closest to the fruit may wither and turn brown, although this doesn't always happen.

The shape of the watermelon should be symmetrical – if it is misshapen it was probably short on water at some point during its growth. 'Thumping' a watermelon is a time-honoured ritual, but most folks don't know what they're listening for, or why. If tapping the fruit gives a sharp metallic sound, the watermelon is not yet ripe. If the sound is muffled, then the melon is ready. And, again, the melon should feel heavy for its size. If you're buying, not picking, a watermelon, you might demand a taste first, as described by Ahmed Tharwat writing recently from Cairo:

> The street peddlers, their donkey carts loaded with big stacks of watermelons, will go around chanting their admiring jingles describing the beauty of their water- melons. 'Hamar we Halawah' (reddish and sweetness), or 'Ya Gammr, ya Gamer' (oh embers, like embers), and the confident watermelon peddler will chant 'Ala Elskinah Ya Helwah', challenging anyone to cut his watermelons and taste them on the spot before buying them.

This method would very likely not be possible at a large super- market!

Both melons and watermelons should be harvested with a sharp knife, leaving a stump at the stem end of the fruit to deter rot. Watermelons should not be harvested in the cool of the morning, as they are prone to cracking then. Melons may be stored in a cool place for a few days for delicate, thin- skinned melons, and a few weeks for thick-skinned melons. Remembering our lessons from the Chain of Being, melons should be washed with soapy water before being cut in order to minimize the possibility of introducing bacteria into the flesh. Melon that has been cut but won't be eaten right away should be stored, covered, in the refrigerator.

Melons can be one of the most delicious foods we eat: sweet as honey, perfumed, luscious, yet cool and thirst-quenching, the perfect melon delights the senses while refreshing our bodies. A Middle Eastern saying goes: 'He who fills his stomach with melons is like he who fills it with light – there is a blessing in them.' I hope that you find many wonderful melons in your future and that, when you eat a melon, you will think a little bit about the incredible journey this fruit has taken across continents, across oceans and across time, to end up on your table. A blessing, indeed.

Appendix II
Ode to the Watermelon

and then
the coolest of all
the planets crosses
the sky,
the round, magnificent,
star-filled watermelon.
It's a fruit from the thirst-tree.
It's the green whale of the summer.
The dry universe
all at once
given dark stars
by this firmament of coolness
lets the swelling
fruit
come down:
its hemispheres open
showing a flag
green, white, red,
that dissolves into
wild rivers, sugar,
delight!
Jewel box of water, phlegmatic

queen
of the fruitshops,
warehouse
of profundity, moon
on earth!
You are pure,
rubies fall apart
in your abundance,
and we
want
to bite into you,
to bury our
face
in you, and
our hair, and
the soul!

Recipes

Armenian Stuffed Melon
(*Missov Sekhi Dolma*)

This dish is very similar to the melon *dolma* reported to have been served in the palaces of the Ottomans. Traditionally lamb would have been the meat used, but modern-day Armenians are fond of pork or a pork/beef combination. You can adjust the amount of sugar depending on your taste and the sweetness of the melon, but to get the true 'Exotic East' flavour, the dish should have some sweetness. Delicious.

2 medium-sized muskmelons
2 (27.5 g) tbsp butter
1 onion, chopped fine
½ lb (225 g) ground lamb, or pork/beef combo
½ cup (100 g) long grain rice
¼ cup (30 g) raisins or currants
¼ cup (30 g) pine nuts (optional)
½ tsp salt
few grinds pepper
¼ tsp cinnamon
2 tbsp sugar
additional ¼ tsp salt
1 cup (225 ml) water
2 tbsp (27.5 g) oil or additional butter

Find the spots where the melons will sit comfortably and slice off the top, just enough to make a 'hat' and give you access to the seed cavity. Scoop out the seeds and strings and discard (or use for *horchata* or *pepitada*). Scoop out about a cup of flesh between the two melons, being sure not to break through the skin. Chop the melon pulp and set aside; set aside the shells and the tops.

In a large skillet melt 2 tbsp butter. Add the onion and ground meat and cook over medium heat until the meat is browned, being sure to break up the meat so it is in small pieces. Add the rice, raisins or currants, pine nuts (optional), salt, pepper and cinnamon and 1 tbsp of the sugar. Stir in the chopped melon pulp. Stir to blend, then stir in the water. Bring to a boil and cover, turn down the heat and simmer until the water is absorbed, about 15 minutes. Taste for salt and pepper and correct the seasoning.

Preheat oven to 375°F (190°C). Sprinkle the remaining 1 tbsp sugar and a bit of additional salt inside the melon shells, then scoop the stuffing inside the melons. If there's stuffing left over you can put it in a greased ovenproof dish and cover with foil. Put the lids on the melons and secure with wooden toothpicks. Oil an appropriately sized baking pan and place the melons in the pan. Put in the middle of the preheated oven and bake for 1 hour. To serve, you may present the entire melons at the table, minus the lids, and give individual servings to your guests. Or cut the melons in the kitchen and arrange the wedges on a serving dish.
Serves 6 as a side dish, 4 as a main course

Mexican Melon Seed *Horchata*

Horchata (Valencian *orxata*) is a Moorish-influenced Spanish drink made from ground seeds, nuts or grains and is related to orgeat. *Horchatas* travelled to Mexico and Latin America with the Spanish and to parts of Greece and Turkey with the Sephardic Jews after the Reconquista. In Spain the drink might be flavoured with vanilla; the Sephardic melon seed *horchata*, which is called *pepitada*, is flavoured with rose or orange-flower water. Most melon *horchatas* (and *pepitadas*) are made with dried and toasted seeds which are crushed, then soaked in water for 36–48 hours. This is a quick, fresh *horchata*, perfect for making right after you've cut open a delicious, new melon. The fresh lime makes it Mexican.

seeds and fibre cut fresh from the core of one sweet melon
(muskmelon, cantaloupe and honeydew all make delicious
horchatas), set aside in a measuring cup
1 cup (225 ml) water for every cup of melon seeds and fibre
1 tbsp sugar for every cup water
juice of 1 lime for every cup water
ice for serving
sprinkle of cinnamon for serving, or a mint sprig

Put the melon seeds and fibre in a blender and add an equal quantity of water by volume, plus the sugar and lime juice. Blend on high until the melon seeds are crushed. Chill the mixture in the blender jar for at least 30 minutes. At serving time, fill a tall glass with ice (crushed is the most delicious) and strain the melon-seed mixture into the glass. Top with a sprinkle of cinnamon or a mint sprig and serve.

Paloodeh
(Persian Melon and Rosewater Smoothie)

Live as if you had never tasted this *paluda*,
As if you know nothing of this kitchen that you have seen,
For its *paluda* cannot help but intoxicate you,
And make you forget your humble sheepskin jacket
and your battered shoes.
Persian poet Rumi (1207–1273)

A *faloodeh* in Iranian these days usually indicates a frozen dessert, but the etymologically related *paloodeh* or *paluda* simply refers to something special and sweet, often involving melons. Azita Mehran's family recipe for this delicious melon drink, which she shares on her delightful blog Turmeric & Saffron, is both special and sweet, a lovely Persian smoothie. It is nice as a refreshing drink on a hot day, but also makes a cooling dessert on a sultry night.

enough orange-fleshed melon to yield four cups
of puréed flesh (usually 1–2 melons)
1 cup (225 ml) cold water
2–3 tbsp sugar or honey
2 tbsp rose water (30 ml)
grated rind of 1 lemon (optional)
mint sprig for garnish (optional)

Wash and clean the melons, cut them in halves, remove the seeds, peel the skin off and cut the melon into small pieces. Put the melon pieces into a blender and add sugar, water, rose water and optional lemon rind. Cover and blend until nearly smooth (a little texture is traditional). Pour into a jug and chill for an hour or two. Serve chilled in glasses either plain or over crushed ice, garnished with the mint sprig if you wish.

Muskmelon Mangoes

The only kind of mangoes most Westerners knew in the nineteenth century were pickled, and yellow muskmelon was often substituted for the mango in the pickle, so much so that 'mangoes' in those days came to mean 'pickled muskmelon'. 'Mangoes' were common in both England and the new United States. This recipe comes from Mary Randolph's *The Virginia Housewife; or, Methodical Cook* (1824).

Oil Mangos

Gather the melons a size larger than a goose egg   put them in a pot, pour boiling salt and water made strong upon them, and cover them up; next day, cut a slit from the stem to the blossom end, and take out the seeds carefully – return them to the brine, and let them remain in it eight days; then put them in strong vinegar for a fortnight, wipe the insides with a soft cloth, stuff them and tie them, pack them in a pot with the slit uppermost; strew some of the stuffing over each layer, and keep them covered with the best vinegar.

To Make the Stuffing for Forty Melons

Wash a pound of white race ginger very clean; pour boiling water on it, and let it stand twenty-four hours; slice it thin, and dry it; one pound of horse-radish scraped and dried, one pound of mustard seed washed and dried, one pound of chopped onion, one ounce of mace, one of nutmeg pounded fine, two ounces of turmeric, and a handful of whole black pepper; make these ingredients into a paste, with a quarter of a pound of mustard, and a large cup full of sweet oil; put a clove of garlic into each mango.

Pickled Watermelon Rind

An old-fashioned classic in North America as well as Russia. Look for thick-skinned watermelons.

1 medium watermelon

2 cups (200 g) pickling salt

4 quarts (4.8 litres) water

1 cup (225 ml) distilled vinegar

3 cups (600 g) white sugar

3 cups (675 ml) water

2 sticks cinnamon

8 whole cloves

1 lemon, thinly sliced, seeds removed

1 tbsp preserved ginger, chopped (12.5 g)

Cut the green skin and the red flesh from the watermelon rind, leaving only the white portion. Cut the white rind into even shapes – either ¾-in. cubes, 1 in. × 2 in. strips, or 1 in. circles. Place into a glass or non-reactive metal bowl and cover with a brine made from combining the salt with the water. Cover and keep in a cool place for at least 8 hours. Drain well, rinse and drain again. Place in a large kettle, cover with cold water, bring to a boil, let simmer for 10 minutes, then drain again, setting the rind aside. Bring the vinegar to a boil in the large kettle, add the sugar and spices except the lemon and ginger, then boil until you have a thick syrup. Skim out the whole spices. Add the rind and the lemon and ginger and bring to a boil again, reduce the heat and simmer for 15–20 minutes or until the rind is translucent. Place in sterilized jars and seal.

Egusi Seed Soup

A classic West African stew/soup, especially popular in Nigeria. Egusi soup is one of those dishes like bouillabaisse that will engender passionate arguments about the 'right' way to make it. Some cooks add tomato; others are horrified by the thought. Some add tripe and fermented locust beans (*iru*), some a smidgeon of curry powder, which is heretical to others. Some like the egusi meal to clump in the finished dish; others prefer it smoothly distributed. A traditional egusi soup will have dried stockfish as part of the base and the meat will include goat and bushmeat. This is a Westernized version, but still fairly authentic. If you can't find egusi seeds or meal, pumpkin seeds may be substituted. Classic recipes do not brown the meat before adding it to the pot.

3 cups (675 ml) water
1-½ lb (675 g) beef stew meat, in bite-sized pieces
1 chicken bouillon cube
1 onion, finely chopped
½ tsp salt
½ cup (110 ml) palm oil or peanut oil
2 large tomatoes, chopped
1 onion, coarsely chopped
1–2 chilli peppers (egusi soup is not blazingly spicy, so adjust the heat to your liking), seeds removed and coarsely chopped
1 lb (450 g) crawfish or shrimp, peeled and cleaned

1 lb (450 g) spinach leaves, cleaned and coarsely chopped
¾ cup (90 g) egusi-seed meal (or egusi or pumpkin seeds
whirled in a blender to a powder) salt, pepper and hot
pepper to taste

Put the water in a large soup pot and add the meat, the bouillon
cube, the onion and the ½ tsp salt. Bring to a boil, turn heat to low
and simmer for 1 to 1 ½ hours until the meat is tender. Heat half
the oil in a large sauté pan, add the tomatoes, the coarsely chopped
onion and the hot pepper and sauté for a few minutes, just until
vegetables are soft. Put them in a blender or food processor and
blend to a coarse paste. Add this mixture to the soup pot, rinse out
the blender with a bit of water and add that to the pot, then let the
soup simmer for another ½ hour. Add the crawfish or shrimp and
let simmer 10 minutes, then stir in the spinach leaves and let simmer another 10 minutes. In the meantime, put the rest of the oil
in a sauté pan over medium heat, add the egusi or pumpkin-seed
meal and sauté for a few minutes, breaking up the clumps or not,
as you prefer. Stir the egusi seed paste into the soup, stir to mix,
again breaking up the clumps or not as you prefer. Let simmer
another 10 minutes. Taste for seasoning and correct. Can be served
as a soup, or over a starch (African yam is traditional, but rice is
good) as a stew.
Serves 6

Watermelon Steak

Some devout vegetarian religions, such as Jainism in India, forbid
adherents from eating watermelon because of its meat-like
appearance, so perhaps the idea of watermelon 'steak' isn't that
far-fetched. Cooked watermelon does indeed take on an entirely
different consistency, losing its crisp granularity and gaining a
silky, yielding texture quite similar to raw tuna.

4 6-ounce (175 g) square cut pieces of watermelon, 1 in. thick,
rind removed or not as you please (the melon will look more

'steak-ish' without the rind)
8 tbsp honey
4 tbsp spiced rum

Poke the watermelon on both sides all over gently with a fork. Drizzle 1 tablespoon honey on each piece of melon. Preheat the grill and grill the watermelon honey side up for 3–5 minutes or until starting to brown. Turn slices over gently and drizzle on the rest of the honey along with the rum and grill for another 3–5 minutes, again until starting to brown. The longer the melon stays under the heat, the silkier and more meat-like will be the texture. Serve hot. (May also be cooked over an outdoor grill, in which case start with the honey side away from the fire to minimize flare-ups.)
Serves 4

Sicilian Watermelon Pudding
(*Gelo di Melone*)

A simple, unusual Sicilian watermelon pudding, clearly showing its 'Arabian Nights' origins. Some people substitute orange-flower water for the cinnamon, and some serve the pudding with whipped cream.

6 cups (900 g) watermelon chunks, rinds and seeds removed
1 cup (200 g) white sugar
½ cup (70 g) cornflour (cornstarch)
⅛ tsp cinnamon
bittersweet chocolate for decorative shavings or use ¼ cup
(30 g) chocolate chips
¼ cup (30 g) green pistachio nuts, chopped
a few jasmine blossoms if you're lucky enough to have them

Put the watermelon chunks in a food processor or blender and purée finely, strain and measure out 5 cups (1.25 litres) of juice. Put half the sugar and all the cornflour in a pot big enough to hold the watermelon juice. Stir the sugar and cornflour, then whisk in the juice, mixing well. Bring the juice mixture to a boil over medium heat, whisking steadily. Once it boils and starts to thicken, beat constantly, making sure to get in the corners. Let boil a minute or two, then take off the heat and whisk in the cinnamon. Pour into individual bowls (clear ones show off the pretty colour) or into an 8' × 8' (20 cm × 20 cm) pan, cover and chill. Just before serving, decorate the top with the chocolate shavings or chips (the chips look more like watermelon seeds but the shavings are easier to eat), pistachio nuts and flowers. Serve to your amazed guests.

Serves 6

Melon Torte à la Scappi

This unusual melon pie is based on one printed in Bartolomeo Scappi's *Opera dell'arte del cucinare* (1570). It tastes quite a bit like a double-crust pumpkin pie, but with a lovely medieval touch. For the pastry 'coffin', a sturdy paste made with flour, eggs, butter and rosewater was called for in the original. I use bought puff pastry, which is not at all authentic but quite delicious. The melon custard can also be baked in a greased tart pan open face, without any crust at all.

2 tbsp butter

4 cups (600 g, or 1 large melon) melon flesh

(I used muskmelon), peeled, seeded and cut into chunks –

a slightly underripe melon is preferred

6 whole eggs

1 cup (225 g) ricotta cheese

1 cup (225 g) cream cheese or mascarpone

¾ cup white sugar (150 g)

¼ cup (30 g) dried breadcrumbs or pounded dried cake

or biscuit crumbs

2 tsp cinnamon

½ tsp finely ground pepper

butter to grease the springform pan
1 tbsp rose water
1 tbsp white sugar
1 tbsp melted butter
sugar and cinnamon for glazing the top
enough pastry for a large springform pan, bottom,
sides and top

Melt the butter in a large skillet, add the melon chunks and sauté over a low heat, turning frequently, until the melon is soft. Let cool a bit. In a large bowl, beat the eggs, ricotta, cream cheese, sugar, breadcrumbs, cinnamon and pepper until well blended. Put the cooked melon in a blender or processor and process until smooth. Add to the egg mixture and beat well.

Preheat the oven to 350°F (190°C). Grease a large springform pan. Line the bottom and sides of the pan with pastry, allowing enough on the sides to meet the lid. Mix the rosewater and 1 tbsp sugar in a small bowl and brush this mixture over the bottom of the pastry. Pour in the custard. Put the 'coffin' lid of pastry on top, crimping the edges to form a tight seal. Pour the melted butter over the top. Bake in the middle of the oven for 1½ hours. Sprinkle a little sugar and cinnamon over the top and bake for an additional 15 minutes. The pie should have risen somewhat and the pastry be browned. Test discreetly in a corner with a sharp knife or cake tester to see if the custard has set. Remove from the oven and let cool. Remove the sides of the springform and serve.
Serves 8–10

Arabian Cardamom-scented Melon Salad

An absolutely delicious salad that is especially beautiful if you use a green- or white-fleshed melon.

½ cup (150 ml) honey
¼ cup (75 ml) lime juice
½ tsp ground cardamom

1 medium *inodorus* sweet melon, such as honeydew or piel de sapo
3 medium oranges
1 pomegranate
sprig of fresh mint for garnish

Put the honey in a small saucepan and bring just to a boil, stirring occasionally. Remove from the heat and allow to cool for a bit, then stir in the lime juice and cardamom. Let cool completely.

Remove the peel and seeds from the melon and cut into bite-sized pieces. Peel the oranges and slice into circles. Remove any seeds. Open the pomegranate and remove the seeds and juice and set aside. Combine the oranges and melon in a bowl, then toss gently with the honey mixture. Chill if desired. Just before serving, sprinkle with the pomegranate seeds and juice, combine gently and garnish with the mint sprig if desired.

Serves 6

Apicius' *Pepones et Melones*

From the late fourth- or early fifth-century Roman cookery classic, *De re coquinaria*. We do not know whether the melons were sweet melons or more cucumberish sorts, nor do we know whether the melons were cooked or served as a salad with the sauce.

Piper, puleium, mel vel passum, liquamen, acetum. interdum et silfi accedit.

Pepper, pennyroyal [a type of mint], honey or passum [condensed wine must or raisin wine], liquamen [roughly like soy sauce or fish sauce] and vinegar; once in a while one adds silphium [no one knows exactly what silphium was, although a type of fennel or asafoetida are suggested].

Greek Watermelon and Feta Salad

I wouldn't be surprised if this were the descendant of Apicius' melon recipe. It is deliciously refreshing on a hot day. Do not let this sit or the salad will get soggy. If you want the melon cold, chill it before you make the salad.

6–7 cups (900–1,050 g) watermelon flesh, seeded, in bite-sized
cubes or balls
1 cup (75 g) fresh mint leaves
⅛ cup (30 ml) balsamic vinegar
freshly ground black pepper
1 cup (175 g) feta cheese, crumbled (a creamy variety is my
favourite here)

Put the watermelon pieces in a bowl. Chop the mint leaves and toss with the melon, then toss again with the vinegar and a few grinds of pepper. Lastly, add the feta and toss quickly and lightly. Serve immediately.

Serves 6

Paharkai Thayir Pachadi
(Bitter Melon in Yoghurt)

This speciality of Tamil Brahmin cooking is a lovely and unusual appetizer or side dish from cookbook author Viji Varadarajan. The spicing, frying and yoghurt all help to tame the inherent bitterness of the melon. The pieces of fried bitter melon should be mixed into the yoghurt just before serving to keep the beguiling crisp texture against the creamy yoghurt.

3 tbsp oil
2½ tbsp oil
2 medium-sized bitter melons (karella)
¼ tsp cayenne pepper or chilli powder
¼ tsp black mustard seeds

2 cups (600 ml) creamy yoghurt
¼ tsp salt

Slice the bitter melons in half and scoop out the seeds and discard. Cut the flesh into thin rounds. Heat 2½ tablespoons oil in a non-stick skillet. Add the bitter melon slices to the oil with the cayenne or chilli powder. Stir-fry for 10–12 minutes over a medium heat, or until the melon is browned and crispy but not burned. In a separate small pan heat the remaining oil. Add the mustard seeds and stir-fry for a minute or two over a medium heat until the seeds start to pop. Put the yoghurt in a bowl and stir in the salt and the popped mustard seeds. Just before serving, stir in the bitter melon.

Serves 6

Melon and Anise Granite

This pairing of melon and anise is common in the south of France and in Catalonia. There, the melon used would probably be a Cavaillon-type cantaloupe. Not having such available, I used half muskmelon and half honeydew, which gave a slightly odd colour, but tasted delicious. Any well-flavoured sweet melon could be used. If the melons are small, the shells make charming and cooling serving dishes; otherwise serve in your prettiest bowls. A very refreshing dish.

½ cup (150 ml) water
½ cup (100 g) sugar
about 2 melons, enough to give 4 cups melon flesh
juice of ½ lemon
4 tbsp (60 ml) anisette

Put the water and sugar in a small saucepan and bring to a boil for about 3–4 minutes, stirring occasionally, making sure all the sugar has dissolved. Set aside to cool. If you're going to use the melon shells as serving bowls, cut the melons in half across the middle

(not from stem to blossom) and scoop out the seeds and discard. Carefully scoop out the melon flesh, getting as close to the rind as possible without piercing it. Wrap the melon shells in aluminium foil and freeze. Put the melon flesh in a blender or food processor. Add the cooled sugar syrup to the melon, along with the lemon juice and anisette. Process or blend until nearly smooth. Pour into a large, shallow baking dish (an aluminium one works best) and freeze uncovered for about 1 hour until crystals start to form. Stir with a fork, working the crystals and mashing, then return to the freezer for about 30 minutes, stir with the fork again. Repeat 2 or 3 more times, until the granite is frozen all over. (This process should take about 3 hours all together.) Fluff with a fork before serving. You may either put it into the frozen shells to serve (the shells will help keep it cold for a few minutes) or serve in bowls.
Serves 8

Martino da Como's Melon Soup

This soup was purportedly a favourite of Pope Paul II, who was said to have died from eating too many melons in 1471. It tastes very medieval and a bit odd, but good. I served it as an appetizer in small cups, both lukewarm and cold, and found it to be quite a conversation starter. The cheese takes the place of salt in this dish.

1 sweet melon, not too ripe (about 4 cups of flesh)
2 tbsp (27.5 g) butter
2 cups (600 ml) chicken stock (broth)
⅛ tsp saffron threads
1 tbsp vinegar
2 eggs
¼ cup (25 g) grated parmesan cheese
¼ tsp freshly grated pepper
1 tbsp white sugar
½ tsp cinnamon

Peel and seed the melon and cut it into bite-sized chunks. Melt the butter in a large skillet over medium heat. Add the melon and sauté, turning it constantly, until the melon is soft. Put the melon pulp into a blender or processor and purée. Put the chicken stock in a medium soup pot and add the melon, bring to a boil, then turn down to a simmer. Crush the saffron threads in your fingers and put them in a small bowl with the vinegar, stirring to let the saffron dissolve a bit. Add to the soup pot. Turn off the heat. Break the eggs into a medium bowl and beat them well with a fork or a whisk, then beat in the cheese. Add ¼ cup (75 ml) broth to the eggs, beating all the while, then another ¼ cup (75 ml), beating, then another ¼ cup (75 ml). The eggs should be warmed and thinned (or tempered) so they do not curdle when added to the soup. When your egg mixture feels at least lukewarm, stir it into the hot melon broth, stirring rapidly and constantly. Put on very low heat and stir constantly, just until the soup thickens, which should happen quickly. Do not allow to boil or the eggs will curdle. Remove from the heat and stir in the pepper, sugar and cinnamon. Taste for seasoning and correct. Serve hot, lukewarm or cold. Do not reheat or the eggs will curdle.

Serves 8

Plugged Melon

The 1910 *Philistine* magazine described what happened after two young girls in the American Southwest sold some melons to railroad passengers: 'Avery Robinson of Louisville had a quart bottle of Kentucky Dew. He showed us a new stunt. He tapped some of the watermelons and poured in a quantity of his antiseptic embalming fluid. When these particular melons were served in the diner, it was explained that they were a new type, evolved by Luther Burbank . . . A preacher tried a slice of the new kind of melon. He liked it and encored. He pronounced it the finest ever. We gave him the address of Luther Burbank, so he could send for the recipe.'

Watermelon is the type of melon 'plugged' most often, since the flesh is so crystalline and absorbs the liquor more easily than sweet melons. In the Wild West bourbon whiskey was the liquor of choice. In the 1960s in the United States that had given way to non-alcoholic ginger ale. You can try anything that suits your fancy, but you might want to try a piece of the melon mixed with your drink of choice first to be sure the combination works.

1 watermelon
about 2 cups (600 ml) chilled champagne (or other alcoholic drink of your choice)

Use a small knife to gently cut a round 'plug', about 1 ½ in. (3 cm) across, in the watermelon. (A square or triangular hole may cause the melon to crack.) Remove the plug and reserve it. Remove a few spoonfuls of the melon flesh using a small spoon or the knife. Using a long thin tool (skewer, knitting needle, etc.), poke around a bit in the melon through the hole – you're trying to make channels so your champagne will penetrate more parts of the melon – but make sure not to poke a hole in the rind. Pour about one cup of the champagne into the hole. Let sit for a minute, then dribble in as much champagne as the melon will take. Replace the reserved plug. If you want to be extra safe, you can tape over the plug. Put the melon in the refrigerator or other cool spot, plug side up, to chill, for at least 2 hours. Remove the tape if you used it, slice the melon and serve.

Select Bibliography

Andrews, Alfred C., 'Melons and Watermelons in the Classical
　　Era', *Osiris*, xii/1 (1956), pp. 368–75
Anthimus, ed. Mark Grant, *De observatione ciborum: On the
　　Observance of Foods* (Totnes, 1996)
Austin, Thomas, ed., *Two Fifteenth-century Cookery-books: Harleian
　　Ms. 279 (AB. 1430), & Harl. Ms. 4016 (AB. 1450), with Extracts
　　from Ashmole Ms. 1429, Laud Ms. 553 & Douce Ms. 55.*
　　(London, 1888)
Azar, Henry, *The Sage of Seville: Ibn Zuhr, His Time and His Medical
　　Legacy* (Cairo, 2008)
Bernier, Francois, *Travels in the Mogul Empire, 1656–1668*, ed.
　　Archibald Constable (London, 1891)
Bottero, Jean, *The Oldest Cuisine in the World: Cooking in
　　Mesopotamia* (Chicago, IL, and London, 2002)
Brothwell, Don, and Patricia Brothwell, *Food in Antiquity*
　　(Baltimore, MD, 1998)
Cable, Alice Mildred, and Francesca French, *Through Jade Gate
　　and Central Asia* (London, 1937)
Carney, Judith, and Richard N. Rosomoff, *In the Shadow of
　　Slavery: Africa's Botanical Legacy in the Atlantic World*
　　(Berkeley, CA, 2010)
Coryat, Thomas, *Coryat's Crudities: Reprinted from the Edition of
　　1611* (London, 1776), vol. II
Dalby, Andrew, *Flavours of Byzantium* (Totnes, 2003)
—, *Food in the Ancient World from A to Z* (London, 2003)

De Candolle, Alphonse, *Origin of Cultivated Plants* (London, 1886)

Decker-Walters, Deena S., 'Cucurbits, Sanskrit and the Indo-Aryans', *Economic Botany*, LIII/1 (1999), pp. 98–112

Goldman, Amy, *Melons for the Passionate Grower* (New York, 2002)

Harvey, John H., 'Gardening Books and Plant Lists of Moorish Spain', *Garden History*, III/2 (1975), pp. 98–112

Hasselquist, Frederick, and Charles Linnaeus, *Voyages and Travels in the Levant in the Years 1749, 50, 51, 52* (London, 1766)

Hehn, Victor, *The Wanderings of Plants and Animals from Their First Home* (London, 1885)

Herlihy, David, *Medieval Culture and Society* (New York, 1968)

Janick, Jules, and Harry S. Paris, 'The Cucurbit Images of the Villa Farnesina, Rome', *Annals of Botany*, XCVII/2 (February 2006), pp. 165–76

Laufer, Berthold, *Sino-Iranica* (Chicago, IL, 1919)

Mavlyanova, R., et al., *Melons of Uzbekistan* (Bioversity International online, 2005)

Nasrallah, Nawal, *Annals of the Caliphs' Kitchen Iby Sayyar al-arraq's Tenth-century Baghdadi Cookbook* (Leiden and Boston, MA, 2007)

National Research Council, *Lost Crops of Africa*, vol. III: *Fruits* (Washington, DC, 2008)

Norrman, Ralf, and John Haarberg, *Nature and Language: A Semiotic Study of Cucurbits in Literature* (London, 1980)

O'Donovan, Edmund, *The Merv Oasis: Travels and Adventures East of the Caspian* (London, 1882), vol. II

Paris, Harry S., et al., 'The Cucurbitaceae and Solanaceae Illustrated in Medieval Manuscripts Known as the *Tacuinum Sanitatis*', *Annals of Botany*, CIII (2009), pp. 1187–205

—, and J. Janick, 'Reflections on Linguistics as an Aid to Taxonomical Identification of Ancient Mediterranean Cucurbits: The Piqqus of the Faqqous', *Cucurbitaceae 2008, Proceedings of the IXth EUCARPIA Meeting on Genetics and Breeding of Cucurbitaceae, Avignon (France)*, 21–4 May 2008, pp. 43–52

—, 'What the Emperor Tiberius Grew in his Greenhouses', *Cucurbitaceae 2008, Proceedings of the IXth EUCARPIA Meeting on*

Genetics and Breeding of Cucurbitaceae, Avignon (France), 21–4
May 2008, pp. 33–42

Pott, D. T., 'Contributions to the Agrarian History of Eastern
Arabia II: The Cultivars', *Arabian Archaeology and Epigraphy*,
v/4 (November 1994), pp. 236–75

Pouncy, Carolyn Johnston, ed., *The Domostroi* (Ithaca, NY, 1994)

Robinson, R. W., and D. S. Decker-Walters, *Cucurbits*
(Wallingford, 1997)

Ruggiero, Laura Giannetti, 'The Forbidden Fruit; or, the Taste
for Sodomy in Renaissance Italy', *Quaderni d'Italianistica*,
XXVII/1 (2006)

Schneewind, Sarah, *A Tale of Two Melons: Emperor and Subject in
Ming China* (Indianapolis, IN, 2006)

Sturtevant, Edward Lewis, 'History of Garden Vegetables',
American Naturalist, XXIII/272 (August 1889), pp. 727–44

Szabó Z., et al., 'Morphological and Molecular Diversity of 47
Melon (*Cucumis melo*) Cultivars Compared to an Extinct
Landrace Excavated from the 15th century', *Cucurbitaceae
2008, Proceedings of the IXth EUCARPIA Meeting on Genetics and
Breeding of Cucurbitaceae, Avignon (France)*, 21–4 May 2008,
pp. 313–21

Wallis, Faith, *Medieval Medicine: A Reader* (Toronto, 2010)

Walters, Terrence W., 'Historical Overview on Domesticated
Plants in China with Special Emphasis on the
Cucurbitaceae', *Economic Botany*, XLIII/3 (1989), pp. 297–313

Watson, Andrew M., *Agricultural Innovation in the Early Islamic
World* (Cambridge, 1983)

Weaver, William Woys, 'Heirloom Melon Varieties', *Mother Earth
News*, www.motherearthnews.com, 20 August 2013

Yang, Si-Lin, and Terrence W. Walters, 'Ethnobotany and the
Economic Role of the Cucurbitaceae of China', *Economic
Botany*, XLVI/4 (1992), pp. 349–67

Zohary, Daniel, and Maria Hopf, *Domestication of Plants in the Old
World* (Oxford, 2004)

Acknowledgements

A thousand thanks to Andy Smith and Michael Leaman for the opportunity to write this book. Especial thanks to editor Martha Jay for her patience, good sense and kindness and to the staff at Reaktion for all their help. Thanks to Dr Harry S. Paris, cucurbit researcher and grower, for patiently answering so many questions. Thanks, as well, to Amy Goldman for her kindness and knowledge, and to Lloyd Bright and Chris Kent for the education and the fun. Andrew Dalby graciously answered my queries, Mike McMahon at the Polyglot Vegetarian fired my curiosity (and answered questions) about melon linguistics. Many people generously offered their time and their work to help me, including Prof. Lise Manniche, Jill Neimark, Chloe Hillier, Claudia Steger (Nunhems), Takashi Itoh, S. M. of Solana Seeds, Juliemar Rosada (National Watermelon Promotion Board), Laurie Jennifer Rizzo (University of Delaware), Craig LeHouillier (North Carolina Tomato Man), Carol Coburn (Town of Ogden, New York), Glenn R. Ford, Irene Lindsey, Sandy Sik Yan Wong, Debra Aubin, Jana Hill (Amon Carter Museum of American Art), Mamiko Suganuma (Suntori), Robert Connan, Ahmed Tharwat, Robert Bly and his assistant Thomas Smith, Azita Mehran and Viji Varadarajan. As always, most special thanks to Ross Petras for support, proofreading, criticism and recipe result testing, among much else. If I've missed anyone, my apologies. And, of course, any errors are mine alone.

Photo Acknowledgements

The author and the publishers wish to express their thanks to the below sources of illustrative material and/or permission to reproduce it:

Carla Antonini: p. 116; courtesy of Baker Creek Heirloom Seed: pp. 22, 26 (Baker Creek Heirloom Seed); © The Trustees of the British Museum, London: pp. 36, 62, 68, 80, 88, 108, 110; The British Library: p. 54; Courtesy Robert Connan: p. 115; Giovanni Dall'Orto: p. 78; Dedda71: p. 63; Dollar Photo Club: pp. 50 (illustrez-vous), 51 (A_Lein), 60 (gaelj), 74 (Vilaty), 95 (axway); courtesy of Glenn R. Ford: p. 31; Peter Forster: p. 92; Glae23: p. 14; Juhan Harm: p. 29; Toby Hudson: p. 18; image by Hutch: p. 21; iStock: p. 6 (Sergey Skleznev); courtesy Takashi Itoh: p. 109; Ji-Elle: p. 72; Judgefloro: p. 27; Katpatuka: p. 20; Library of Congress, Washington, DC: pp. 59, 101, 107; Los Angeles County Museum of Art: p. 35; courtesy of Lise Manniche: p. 38; The Metropolitan Museum of Art: pp. 67, 102; Sakurai Midori: p. 17; National Gallery of Art, Washington, DC: p. 77; Olaff-pomona: p. 10; Veronique Pagnier: p. 114; Ralf Roletschek: p. 19; Ton Rulkens: p. 23; courtesy of Solana Seeds: p. 24; The State Museum of Fine Arts of Georgia, Tbilisi: p. 83; courtesy Special Collections, University of Delaware Library: p. 12; The Walters Art Museum: pp. 32, 53; courtesy Watermelon.org: p. 11; Wellcome Library, London: p. 98; courtesy Sandy Sik Yan Wong, www.gardeningoncloud9.com: p. 39.

Index

italic numbers refer to illustrations; **bold** to recipes